YOUR VOTE IS MAGIC!

To Eden -
always remember . !
your Vote is Magic !

Love

[i]

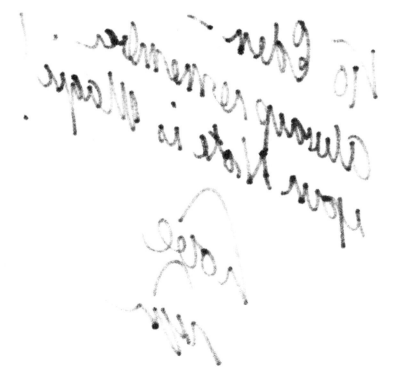

Your Vote Is Magic!

How a Donkey, an Elephant, and an Illusionist
Are Making Voters Appear

By

Lyn Dillies

Lovebug Publishing
Westport, Massachusetts

Library of Congress Control Number: 2012906375
CIP data for this book are available from the Library of
Congress
ISBN: 978-0-615-66530-6

Cover Design: Chris Williams
Cover photography: Judy Ballantine
Research consultant: Patricia Millman
Subtitle inspiration: Megan Stubbs
Printed in the United States of America

Dedication

This book is dedicated to my parents, who have always been the real magic in my life.

To my mother, who is my hero and best friend.

And to my father, who never had the chance to fully know how much he inspired me and whose impact is with me every day.

I don't know what I would have done without them. Thank goodness they always had the time and patience to watch one of my tricks just one more time . . . "Can you watch it once more?" I would ask. They never said no.

I will be forever grateful.

Acknowledgements

A very special thank you to Patricia Millman for giving me the confidence, guidance and support to write this book. You helped make this book a reality!

Thank you to Abner and Emily for being such wonderful animals. May you always know how much you are loved.

Thank you to Judy Ballantine for entrusting your beloved donkey, Abner, to me and the Buttonwood Park Zoo.

Thank you to Shara Crook Martin, Dr. William Langbauer, Bill Sampson and all of the trainers at the Buttonwood Park Zoo: Jenny, Kay, Sarah, and Shelly for your expertise, patience and diligence. It will always be deeply appreciated!

Thank you to my assistant Marc Leblanc and technical director Steve Zakszewski for always coming through, no matter how outlandish or challenging my brainstorms are!

Thank you to Ron Fortier for all of your hard work, never-wavering support and help with my vision.

Thank you to Mayor Lang for enabling Your Vote Is Magic! to happen and believing in my message.

Thank you to Mayor Kalisz for being the original catalyst in my work with Emily and Ruth.

Thank you to Phil Paleologos, Ken Pittman, and Ellen Ratner for hosting *Your Vote Is Magic!* You added your own magic to the evening!

Thank you to Maria Tomasia for your enthusiasm and help to promote Your Vote Is Magic!

Thank you to Bill Webster for your constant belief in my dream.

Thank you to all of the volunteers and crew involved in the illusion. I hope you never forget how you helped make the impossible possible.

Thank you to the maintenance workers of the Buttonwood Park Zoo for always going above and beyond for us.

Thank you to David Oliver for your talent, creativity and friendship. You are amazing in so many ways.

Thank you to Dave Lebeau from Lightworks Productions for your generosity.

Thank you to my music composer, Joe Carrier, for your beautiful score.

Thank you to Senator Michael Rodrigues for exemplifying the importance of our vote.

Thank you to Anne Marie Couto and Kirks Follies for coming to my fashion rescue!

Thank you to Sue Weiner for all of your help.

Thank you to ALPS for providing such exceptional production and service.

Thank you to all the participants in the Your Vote Is Magic! rally: girl scouts, servicemen, veterans, and performers . . . you made it all the more special.

Thank you to Lee's Market for supplying grapes to Emily and Ruth. You kept them very happy!

Thank you to my film director, John Methia, for working your magic!

Thank you to my photographer, John Robson, for capturing how special the event was.

Thank you to the bravery of all the souls who had the passion to fight for what they believed in—the right to vote.

Thank you to my Aunt Rozzie for her inspiration and for giving me the courage to pursue my career in magic.

Thank you to my Aunt Nat for being the best clapper in the audience and never missing a local show.

Thank you to my cousin Martha for all of your help and support with Your Vote Is Magic! and for being such an important part of my life.

Thank you to my dear friend Ken. You will always be part of my magic.

Thank you to all of my pals in magic including "Uncle Ray," General Grant, Andre Kole, Dantini, and the late Larry White—for your friendship and wonderful support through the years.

And my most profound thanks to my family and friends for being there . . . ALWAYS! You are cherished more than you'll ever know!

Table of Contents

Introduction

I don't claim to be an expert on voting or even an eloquent writer. I'm a professional Illusionist who set out to perform an amazing, original illusion with a message. This book is written purely from my heart to tell my story about that illusion, called Your Vote Is Magic! One of my goals through this endeavor has always been to help educate, motivate and inspire as many students as possible about voting. I hope my book will navigate a way through their high-tech world and instill in them the importance of their future vote. *Your Vote Is Magic!* has been written through the eyes of an average citizen. As you will see, I was compelled to present a really grand, unique illusion for the 2008 presidential election. Through my father's beliefs I knew early on just how important voting is. That's what I hope to pass along. As I ventured through my journey, it was an eye-opener for me to realize just how much voting really affects our everyday lives. And so it became more than a book—it became an exciting adventure.

Your Vote Is Magic! will engage the reader from the conception of the illusion, as it follows the process of creating one of the most elaborate illusions ever performed in the world of magic. Although there will still be a large element of mystery (that's guaranteed!), I'll actually reveal what it took to make it happen, in its many fascinating, sometimes very stressful, and often funny details.

I hope this book will be a page-turner because that's how the process felt to me for an entire year, as the concept was becoming a reality, with all of it leading to one fabulous night and the heart-stopping reality of live performance.

The reaction to the illusion Your Vote is Magic! has been gratifying and very varied. People often asked me *how* I did it. Some people have even asked me *why* I did it. To that question I say that my motivation has always been crystal clear: to make a difference!

May the readers of this book become as enlightened as I have been about this incredible gift and never be "too busy" or "too skeptical" to get out and vote!

CHAPTER 1

THE EARLY YEARS

A thousand pairs of eyes were focused on me. I was about to present a king-sized magical illusion—performed live—before this excited crowd. The enormous effort of many talented people and amazing luck along the way had led to this moment. I knew, as with any live performance, there was always the possibility of the unexpected.

With my crew in position and attentively awaiting their cues, I began: "To celebrate our freedom to vote, I've created something a little special . . ."

If you had known me as a young girl, the notion of me growing up to become a professional illusionist would have seemed totally impossible. I was born in the city of New Bedford, Massachusetts, the daughter of Loretta and Calvin Dillies. As far back as I can recall, I was painfully shy. I never raised my hand in class to answer a question and would hide behind my parents when introduced to someone new. It seems ironic to think back to my first magic show experience. I was eight years old when I watched an elderly vaudeville-style magician perform in my elementary school auditorium. I was so nervous that he might pick me as a volunteer to go onstage that I slid way down in my seat so he wouldn't see me. The good thing was that he could have never spotted me, but the bad thing was I never saw the show!

When I was ten years old, my parents and I moved to a lovely, small town called Westport, Massachusetts. I left the Hathaway Elementary School in New Bedford and was now enrolled in the Westport Middle School. Even though I didn't enjoy my elementary school experience very much because I was so shy, it was a piece of cake compared to my new school. At least I had a couple of good friends in my old school. At the new school, I was bullied for the first few years and consequently detested going to school every day. In the Westport Middle School, I felt like I was thrown into a pack of wolves. I would come home every day with a headache or stomach ache. Fortunately, I lived in a wonderful neighborhood and made some good friends, one of whom is still a best friend today. My nickname in the hood was "pick," short for toothpick because of my very slender build. Little did I know how that slender build would serve me for my future career!

Perhaps a seed was planted when I experienced that first magic show from my sunken chair position, because at twelve years old I watched a television show called "The Magician," starring the late Bill Bixby. He played the part of a magician who owned a private jet and used his magic to fight crime. I was thoroughly intrigued by his magic, enough so that my father took me to a local magic shop. He bought me a few tricks that were small enough to fit in one's pocket. I practiced and practiced until they were perfected and then brought them to school with me. It felt so natural for me to be showing the tricks in the lunchroom, in class, and even on the school bus. Lo and behold, I started making friends and becoming a little popular. The magic was so empowering for me. It all just clicked and totally transformed my life.

Now, I couldn't wait to come home from school to work on my magic. I was consumed with it. I read lots of magic books and made most of my own tricks. All of my school notebooks had scribbles and doodles of tricks I wanted to perform or create. I walked up and down the local highway collecting aluminum cans to turn in for money. Counting every penny, I made a "wish list" of tricks I wanted to buy. After a while, I began to walk around my neighborhood carrying a cardboard box containing homemade tricks, then I'd ring a neighbor's doorbell and ask if he or she would like to see a show. After being welcomed in, I'd set up a TV table in their living room, do my little show, pack up and walk to the next house. I'm sure that after a few months, when the doorbell rang my neighbors would hide and pretend that they weren't home!

Finally, after saving all my money, I had enough to buy my first big professional trick. The cost was $50.00. When I went to the magic shop to purchase it, I was so nervous about spending that amount of money that I passed out cold. If I knew then how much money a big illusion show would cost to put together today, I would have never gotten up off the floor!

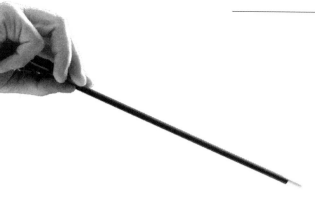

CHAPTER 2

A LOVE OF PERFORMING

Nobody will ever deprive the American people of the right to vote except the American people themselves, and the only way they could do this is by not voting.
Franklin D. Roosevelt

started performing for birthday parties, scout groups, and nursing homes to gain experience. My first professional gig was doing a show for the Eastern Star, a Masonic group in New Bedford. My mother drove me there in her station wagon. She helped carry in my cardboard boxes loaded with props and set them up backstage. I had them all lined up on a long table. After presenting a trick, I'd run backstage and hand it to my mother, as she gave me the next trick. I'd exclaim, "They really liked that one! Did you hear them clap?"

Before every show, I'd be a nervous wreck—but afterwards I felt like I had conquered the world. All these years later, I still feel the same way before and after every show. I just knew in my early teens that I was destined to do magic. I lived and breathed it.

In my sophomore year, *Scholastic Magazine* did a story on me. They sent a reporter and photographer from New York City to interview me one day, and the next day they covered me doing a show on Cape Cod. I ended up being in a filmstrip and magazine that *Scholastic* produced featuring children pursuing unusual hobbies. A segment was televised on CBS National News. My parents were getting calls from family and friends around the county. It was a pretty neat thing back then. The reporter from *Scholastic*, Jane Startz, has become a highly acclaimed executive producer of award-winning family films.

In my junior year of high school, I remember meeting my guidance counselor, Mr. Melli, to discuss my future career plans. Without batting an eye, I told Mr. Melli that I was going to become a fulltime professional illusionist. He looked at me as if I had three heads and advised me to have a serious backup plan. I am so grateful that I've never had to use a Plan B. Years later, I was so flattered when Mr. Melli called me to perform my show on Career Day for the school and talk to the students about following their dreams. A few years ago, I was deeply touched and honored to be asked to deliver the commencement speech at Westport High School, my Alma Mater. Talk about full circle.

Lyn, 14 years old, at one of her first performances.

CHAPTER 3

FAMILY AND FRIENDS

Our democracy is but a name. We vote? What does that mean? It means that we choose between two bodies of real, though not avowed, autocrats. We choose between Tweedle-dum and Tweedledee.
Helen Keller

I t's taken me many years to get my "act" together and actually perform the show I had always envisioned. I've wanted my show to be a complete theatrical experience, including spectacular illusions, audience participation, comedy, and great lighting—and to make it entertaining as well as delivering high-quality magic that an entire family can enjoy. There have been many "hard knocks" along the way. For every highlight of my career, there have been a hundred disappointments. But with a tremendous amount of help from my parents, family, and friends, I'm extremely fortunate that I've been able to live my dream.

I've had an incredible support system through the years. When I started out, my aunts, including my Aunt Rozzie and Aunt Nat, would help with any sewing that had to be done. My mother was my driver, secretary, bookkeeper and backstage helper. My cousin Martha would sometimes step in as my assistant and, in recent years, her children, Megan and Sarah, whom I consider my "nieces," have also helped onstage and with special projects. My Uncle Freddie would help make some of the props with his superb carpentry skills, and of course, my father, Calvin, was invaluable, being a master electrician with many other mechanical talents. There are too many projects he helped me with to count. Sometimes he'd stay up all night figuring out a better way to make something work.

2001: Lyn and her father, Calvin, in Las Cruces, New Mexico. He accompanied her truck driver to see her performances with the Las Cruces Symphony.

2002: Cape Cod. Lyn's Aunt Nat, father Calvin, mother Loretta, and Aunt Rozzie help with tickets and merchandising at a show.

I'll never forget the first illusion he made for me. He knew how badly I wanted to perform Harry Houdini's "Metamorphosis, which involved a wooden crate. One day he came home with a chest he purchased from an antique store. Of course I knew how the illusion worked, but I had no clue how we were going to modify this old trunk and turn it into a miracle. Well, my father's ingenuity made it happen. The method was brilliant. Now that I look back on that old trunk that I still have, it reminds me of how much my father loved me and would stop at nothing to help me attain my dream. When I purchased my most recent truck, he helped spec it out from the kind of engine I needed to all of the polished aluminum trim. How many fathers do you know who would be so proud that their daughter's truck was bigger than theirs?

Incidentally, "Metamorphosis" has become a signature illusion in my show, and it is actually the grand finale. Since the original trunk my father revamped, I have had a few trunks professionally built. "Metamorphosis" is an illusion Harry Houdini made famous. I discovered it when the late illusionist Doug Henning featured it in "The Magic Show" on Broadway and later in his touring show.

In my presentation, a wooden crate is shown empty. My assistant, Marc Leblanc, climbs inside the box and I place shackles and padlocks on his wrists. Next, he steps into a cloth sack and I tie it at the top with a rope. With Marc inside, I place the lid on the crate and padlock all four sides. There is a cloth hoop which fits around the outside of the crate. I jump onto the crate and quickly bring the curtained hoop up to my shoulder height. This takes approximately two seconds. I toss the hoop in the air and it barely clears my head. Within a millisecond I have vanished and Marc has caught the hoop. It happens instantaneously and looks like trick photography. Marc jumps off the box, unlocks all the padlocks, opens up the box and I am now in the cloth sack, which is still tied. When Marc unties the sack, the locked shackles are on my wrists and I have completely changed my costume. Marc quickly unlocks the handcuffs, and after he lifts me out of the box, we do a final pose and there are colored confetti explosions that match my costume change which has been red, white and blue since 9/11.

I recently performed for a private party and someone came up to me afterwards and told me she had hired me to perform at her son's birthday party many, many years ago. I was just starting out as a young teenager and she remembered my mother driving me to the show and running the tape recorder for the music. It was a precious memory and another reminder that my mother has also been by my side every step of the way.

CHAPTER 4

"MAGIC AT THE SYMPHONY"

Thinking is not to agree or disagree. That is voting.
Robert Frost

I t's taken almost a lifetime to attain the success for which I've strived. I've had the privilege of working with many celebrities, including Mikhail Baryshnikov, Crystal Gayle, Jeff Dunham, and Richard Jeni, to name a few. I've had the good fortune of appearing on Fox-TV News, CBS-TV News, The Discovery Channel, and The Statler Brothers Show. I'm very humbled to have played some of the most prestigious venues in the country, including The Magic Castle, The Belk Center, The Carpenter Center for the Performing Arts, The Ford Center for the Arts, The United Nations, The Showboat Hotel, Trump Plaza, and The Manhattan Center. I've made magic history twice for my work with elephants, and have appeared nationally in a print ad. I have to say, however, that of all the exciting things I've accomplished in my career, I am most proud of my "Magic At The Symphony" program.

I inherited my deep love and appreciation of classical music from my grandfather, Kenneth Park, a professional violinist and music director of the New Bedford public school system. He also taught private lessons and, much to his delight, taught me how to play the violin. I can still remember how exciting it was to watch my grandfather play first violin under the baton of Arthur Fiedler, the legendary conductor of the Boston Pops. But one of my most cherished memories of him are the times we played duets. Every Christmas Eve, he and I would play carols on our violins for the rest of the family.

Every day after school, I would stay at my grandparents' home while waiting for my mother to pick me up after work. I would be surrounded by such beautiful classical music played by my grandfather as he was practicing. Inspired by

Lyn and her grandfather, Kenneth Park, playing a Christmas duet together. Lyn's father, Calvin, is in background "conducting" and cousin, Martha holds the Christmas carol book.

those memories, I created a unique program that combines my magic with a live, full symphony orchestra. The symphony is onstage behind me playing classical music for my illusions. It's an exhilarating, breathtaking concert that brings the music to life with my magic. The magic enhances the music and the music enhances the magic. It's a wonderful way for symphonies to introduce classical music to new audiences, particularly children.

Creating "Magic At The Symphony" took countless hours of listening to the various selections of classical music to decide which piece to use for what illusion. I wanted every crescendo of the music to coincide with every dramatic moment of the illusion. I also wanted to integrate the conductor into the show, so I conjured up an illusion at the beginning of the program to magically make him appear. He also learns a magic trick during the presentation.

After my symphony manager Robert Gewald and I marketed the concept to various orchestras, we had no idea where we'd have our first booking. It was a novel idea and sometimes symphonies are very hesitant to try anything new. Personally, I thought our first engagement would be with a small regional symphony.

The answer to that question took almost a full year of waiting. Well, one day in the summer of 1999, on my birthday, I was with one of my best friends in NYC visiting her daughter. She asked me what was going on with the "symphony project." I told her we were so frustrated because it hadn't gotten off the ground yet. Later that afternoon, Mr. Gewald called and told me we were going to premier "Magic At The Symphony" at Lincoln Center in New York City!

And there I was in New York City receiving the news! I arranged to see the stage at Avery Fisher Hall the next day. It was a gorgeous hall and the acoustics were impeccable. My legs were shaking as I walked onto the stage. The hall seats three thousand people.

My father arranged a bus for sixty family members, friends and fans to attend the premier. It was a sold-out house. Knowing how proud my parents were sitting in the audience was one of the most memorable moments of my career.

"Magic At The Symphony" has now appeared with some of the most prominent symphonies in the country, including the Utah Symphony, San Diego Symphony and Virginia Symphony. We currently have an engagement pending with the Boston Pops. One of my next projects is to turn "Magic At The Symphony" into a television special, to educate children about classical music and the symphony as well, utilizing my magic as the visual hook. Stay tuned . . .

1999: New York City. Lyn and her proud parents, Calvin and Loretta after her performance at Lincoln Center.

A poster of a performance with the Wichita Symphony.

CHAPTER 5

FOLLOW YOUR DREAM

If we took away woman's right to vote, we'd never have to worry about another Democratic President.
Ann Colter

I can honestly say that there isn't anything more thrilling than performing in front of a live audience. I've always taken the responsibility of delivering a show I can be proud of and being a role model very seriously. As I sometimes tell children as part of a question-and-answer session after a school assembly, I believe we are all born with a gift. I say, "It's that special something inside of us that allows us to inspire and touch people's lives. You may not know what your gift is right now, but that's okay, because in time, it can't help but appear. It's part of who you are. And when you do discover what your gift is, make sure you unwrap it and share your own magic with the world." I go on to explain to them how lucky I was to know, at a very young age, what my gift was. But we all have one, whether it's becoming a teacher, a nurse, a doctor, or a bus driver—whatever the dream—be passionate about it and do it with everything in your heart.

Every time I am on a stage, I am so thankful that I can still carry out my dream. I never take it for granted because I understand how fragile life is and that it can change in an instant. I'm humbled to read letters I have received that I've been able to make a difference in people's lives, especially the lives of children. It's so rewarding and heartening to know that my magic can have an impact.

But I've always hoped that somehow, someday my

magic could transcend the stage, that it could be used for something more meaningful, and serve a greater purpose. After you read about the Your Vote Is Magic! journey, I hope you will understand the passion behind the message and feel that it is indeed something we should all embrace.

CHAPTER 6

AN ABSOLUTE BRAINSTORM

The minimum, the very basic minimum, of a citizen's duty is to cast a vote on election day. Even now, too few of us discharge this minimal duty. By such negligence, such indifference, such sheer laziness, we discard, unused, a gift and a privilege obtained for us at a gigantic cost and sacrifice.

Eleanor Roosevelt

Summer 2007 - The Brainstorm

I knew that the 2008 presidential election would be a very historic one. Whenever a significant election came along, it would remind me of how passionate my father felt about voting. My earliest memory of my father getting me involved in a campaign was when I was around eight years old. He was the campaign manager for George Clark, who was running for re-election as City Councilor in New Bedford, MA. We were buying up every single package of Clark gum from all of the stores downtown. I would staple each piece to a promo postcard about George Clark. We'd hold political signs and hand out a postcard to anyone walking by. The slogan we'd say was, "STICK with Clark." Maybe that's what helped George Clark get re-elected or, perhaps, it was due to my father being a great campaign strategist.

My father believed that people working together could create change. In later years, he became concerned that the country was starting to become apathetic. He always instilled in me how important it was to vote and to take that right very seriously. I remember hearing a story about a local politician, Michael Rodrigues, who was running for State Representative. It was an extremely close race. My father worked on his campaign and stood by as they recounted the votes. The winner, Michael Rodrigues, was determined by seven votes. He has gone on to become State Senator.

One of the many candidates Lyn's father, Calvin, actively campaigned for was Selectman Claude Ledoux.

*Calvin Dillies served as District Attorney Paul Walsh's Campaign Manager. Here, they cele-
brate his victory.*

One day in late summer of '07, a few years after my father passed away, I had a vision of performing an incredible, never-before-attempted illusion that would be an exciting, visual statement to empower voters. I would create a public service campaign, then a live voter rally, and the illusion would be the finale. It would be called Your Vote Is Magic!

Now, how was I going to accomplish this feat? I had the basic idea for the illusion. It would be a major, ramped-up version of something I had done eight years earlier in New Bedford, Massachusetts. Only this time, instead of producing two elephants in succession, my dream was to produce the live mascot of each respective political party: a donkey to represent the Democratic Party and an elephant to represent the Republican Party.

When I came up with the concept for the illusion, I knew there would be many speed bumps in the road ahead. The first and foremost question was, where should it be performed? My heart instantly told me to present it at the Buttonwood Park Zoo in New Bedford. I could have opted to present it in a much larger city and avoided some of the potential stumbling blocks, but from my experience of performing the illusion eight years earlier, it would have still required ten to fourteen days of working with the large truss framework, which was the structural part of the illusion, not to mention training the animals, which is a tremendous undertaking. The expense to physically mount the illusion would have been the same no matter where it was performed.

It's also not an easy task to find an elephant and a donkey. To rent these animals would have cost approximately $7,000 per day. If they were professionally trained, it still would have taken at least three to four days to get the choreography and timing down. And as far as using animals from another zoo, it would have been nearly impossible to have the zoo's permission without having any prior experience working with their animals.

If we could pull it together, ideally, then performing the illusion in New Bedford would be great for the city as well as the Buttonwood Park Zoo. I had a real soft spot for the Zoo, the staff and, of course, their elephants. And being born in New Bedford and having lived there for 10 years held very special meaning for me.

So, first thing on the agenda was to ask the Zoo if it would be interested in taking on this mammoth project. Because of my history of working with their two resident elephants, Emily and Ruth, over the years, I was thankful that there was a high level of trust. First, I met with Shara Martin Crook, who is the Zoo's curator. Shara and I had worked together on the last two elephant milestones. Not only was Shara a former elephant keeper, but she is also a veterinary technician. Shara has always been very supportive of my ideas, however outlandish they seemed! Shara, the staff, and I were always so thrilled to see how much the various illusions benefited "the girls" (Emily and Ruth). It made us happy to see how much they enjoyed the training and enrichment process. But I've learned to never take anything for granted, and knowing that this was going to be a whole different dynamic with the two species of animals, I decided I wouldn't get my hopes up too much.

I met with Shara and she said she was "game" but, as she expressed, "I thought it was an interesting idea, because the idea of having two different animals in close proximity was going to be really challenging. Having had so much success with the previous illusions, we knew what we were in for, as far as working with the animals and the careful training process. But having a donkey in the mix was so different. First of all, how would we introduce the animals to each other and get the animals near each other? And where would we house a donkey? And what elephant would handle it better? There were lots of questions to ask." Shara had confirmed what I was fearing. The Zoo did not have a donkey in its collection.

Shara kindly arranged a meeting with Bill Sampson, the Head Animal Keeper. Bill was very enthusiastic as well. He and Shara both felt it would be a very positive experience for some of the newer animal keepers who had never been involved with our past projects. Shara and Bill had to give some thought as to which elephant would do the illusion. Both agreed that Emily would be best suited for the feat. So they lined up the keepers and we met to discuss our plan. Fortunately, the animal keepers were very excited about the idea as well, but, of course, had some trepidation. Jenny Theuman, one of the Zoo's elephant keepers who would train Emily, said, "It was an awesome chance to do some really fun enrichment, and what a cool opportunity to try some different thinking outside of the box. It was a fresh, new idea."

Sarah Fleurent, another animal keeper of the Zoo, who would became the donkey's trainer, said, "It was a great idea but from an animal standpoint I thought it was an overwhelming idea. I just knew it was going to be a lot of work on our part, but definitely it was a great idea." And Kay Santos, the zookeeper and elephant keeper who became involved with various facets of the training process said, "I thought it would be really cool, but initially I wasn't sure how it was going to work and how Emily was going to react to a donkey."

So the donkey was definitely the X factor for everyone. We knew it wasn't going to be easy to accomplish, especially without having a clue about what donkey would be used. Our other major concern was how the donkey would get along with Emily the elephant. Sarah thought because Emily can be a little "touch and go," it might be hard to get her to stand next to a donkey, and she was concerned about someone getting hurt. Jenny wondered if Emily would be okay with the donkey, and also if she would be okay without having her elephant gal pal, Ruthie, nearby. Back in 2000, both elephants, Emily and Ruth, were involved with the original illusion, but now it would be just Emily. As Jenny stated, "Emily is the dominant personality when it comes to the two of them. It's interesting though, that when Emily gets scared or nervous, she'll hide behind Ruth for comfort. Emily can be a bully sometimes, but the dynamic is the opposite when she's scared. So my concern was, will she be okay with the donkey, and will she be okay without Ruth."

Knowing from experience how incredibly talented the animal keepers were with their training capabilities, I had total confidence in their expertise and felt certain that we should move forward. All the new trainers would rely on Shara and Bill's guidance. But now, one of many hurdles developed. Because the Zoo is owned by the city of New Bedford, I had to have permission from the new mayor, Scott Lang. I had a great relationship with his predecessor, Mayor Kalisz, but didn't know Mayor Lang that well. Another potential snag was that there was a new Zoo director, who wouldn't be starting until January of 2008. Even assuming the mayor said yes, I would still need his blessing.

For an entire year, any free time I had when not performing and promoting my show was dedicated to Your Vote is Magic! One thing I learned along the way was that no one, absolutely no one, had the same passion and vision as I had for this project because it was so deeply personal. I had to continue to take the reins and run with it. Spending so much time in the New Bedford, MA, area, and even near the elementary school I had attended, brought me back to my childhood. I would be reminded of that thin, unpopular, painfully shy girl, who dreaded going to school and now, fast forward, many, many years later to Lyn Dillies, "America's Premier Female Illusionist," taking on animals, a mayor, a city, red tape, and a zoo. It was mind boggling!

Now, in the meantime, while waiting to get through some red tape (and by the way, why is it always red?), I knew I had to work on finding a donkey. As I learned from my meeting at the Buttonwood Park Zoo, they did not have a resident donkey. If I couldn't find one, there was no sense in moving forward. After doing some research, I discovered the Donkey/Mule Society and joined. Once accepted, I put out the word that I was looking for a donkey for a very special project. Unbelievably, in a few days, I had a couple of responses, which led to this wonderful lady, Judy Ballantine, from Dover, Massachusetts. She was active in the Save Your Ass Long Eared Rescue and the Yankee Donkey and Mule Society. Judy was so enthusiastic about the illusion and its message. She also thought that working with an elephant and donkey sounded like a fantastic idea. I drove to her house to meet her and was introduced to her beautiful, large, standard donkey, Abner. Abner was about nine years old and Judy had owned him for about a year. Supposedly, Abner had been a pack donkey from out West and had never been ridden. She had been working with him a lot so she was very familiar with his personality and tolerance for certain situations. Judging by his demeanor the day I met him, I thought he would be just great. Abner was so sweet and absolutely gorgeous. He would make a very striking mascot. Judy said he could go to the Zoo anytime and stay as long as necessary. I had to pinch myself. Was this lady for real? Here was Judy, meeting me, a total stranger and she was offering to let her beloved animal leave home for a few months to learn some magic. What a neat lady. I knew we'd be friends for life!

Cool. I now had permission from the Zoo and I had a donkey to use. Now to arrange a meeting with the mayor. With a little finagling, I managed to get an appointment. Then, something came up at the last minute and the appointment had to be rescheduled. And after another rescheduled appointment (of course my project wasn't exactly a priority with a mayor running a major city), I couldn't believe how much anxiety I had about asking him for permission. I felt like so much was riding on his reaction. I had waited weeks for this moment. And if he said no, then it would end all chances of it happening in New Bedford. Deep breath.

After proposing the concept about promoting voter awareness and utilizing the Zoo and animals to make a big visual impact, he said YES—as long as it was kept non-partisan. I told him not to worry. We would make sure it would be totally non-partisan. Thankfully, Mayor Lang was very excited and offered his full support. Yippee - another big victory!

Now I had to wait another three weeks for the new director to get settled in with the Zoo. The good thing was that Mayor Lang personally hired the new director and, after doing a little checking, he seemed very progressive and loved elephants. Dr. William Langbauer, the new director of the Buttonwood Park Zoo, actually had conducted a lot of research in the wild, learning about how elephants can communicate with each other using infrasound. I was hoping he would be as enthused as Mayor Lang and see the value in this undertaking.

CHAPTER 7

WHY A DONKEY AND AN ELEPHANT?

Half of the American people have never read a newspaper. Half never voted for President. One hopes it is the same half.

Gore Vidal

You may be wondering about the political significance of a donkey and elephant? The donkey and elephant are the mascots of our two major political parties. But how did all of this start? And what is a political party? A political party is an organization of people who share common political beliefs. In the United States, the two most prominent political parties are the Democrats and the Republicans. Each party seeks to control and influence the government. Consequently, party members try to win public support and votes for issues that matter to them and also to elect their slate of political candidates. There are some gray areas, however, within the parties' differences. Sometimes their policies overlap and their philosophies aren't always clear cut. The Republican Party is traditionally known for being "right" and "conservative" and the Democratic Party is known for being "left" and "liberal." However, each party has a strong middle base.

Back in the late 1700s, the Democratic Party was formed. It started as the Democratic/Republican Party. Then, in 1824, it split into different groups, one of which was the Democratic Party. Andrew Jackson was largely responsible for its emergence. When Jackson was running for president in 1828, his opponents tried to portray him as a "jackass" for his strong-willed beliefs and slogan, "Let the people rule." Mr. Jackson was amused by the concept and turned a potentially damaging situation to his advantage. He used the donkey image in his campaign advertising.

Then an extremely popular political cartoonist of the time, Thomas Nast, used his satiric skill so effectively that he is generally credited with making the donkey the recognized symbol of the Democratic Party. That happened in 1870. Thomas Nast was born in Germany and moved with his family to New York City when he was six years old. He was artistically talented at an early age. Because of his upbringing in New York City, he became politically and socially savvy and incorporated those traits into his drawings. In 1862, he starting working at *Harper's Weekly Newspaper*. His cartoon of the donkey first appeared in a *Harper's Weekly* issue and was supposed to represent an anti-Civil War faction. The public latched onto it and by 1880 the donkey had become the unofficial mascot of the Democratic Party. The donkey mascot wasn't the only one that gained notoriety from Thomas Nast cartoons.

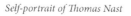

Self-portrait of Thomas Nast

[41]

"A LIVE JACKASS KICKING A DEAD LION."

And such a Lion! and such a Jackass!

The original Nast illustration of the donkey that became the official mascot for the Democratic Party.

"A Live Jackass Kicking a Dead Lion," Harper's Weekly Magazine, January 15, 1870. Thomas Nast Illustrations, Library of Congress

This was the original Nast illustration of the elephant that would become the official mascot of the Republican Party. "Third-Term Panic," by Thomas Nast, originally published in Harper's Weekly Magazine, November 1874. Thomas Nast Illustrations, Library of Congress

Since Roman times, the elephant has been symbolized as a sign of strength. Thomas Nast, a staunch Republican, purposely chose the elephant to represent the Republican Party because of its attributes, including its size and intelligence. It made its first appearance in his November 7, 1874, cartoon called, "The Third Term Panic." The phrase related to the fears people had about President Grant running for a third term. Nast continued using the elephant icon in other cartoons and it soon became the mascot of the Republican Party. Other cartoonists adopted the symbols as well for their illustrations.

Besides Thomas Nast, another of our greatest political cartoonists was Clifford K. Berryman. Berryman is credited with promoting the enduring and beloved "Teddy" Bear, a symbol associated with President Theodore Roosevelt.

Berryman was one of Washington's best-known political cartoonists in the first half of the 20th century. He drew for the *Washington Post* from 1890 until 1907, and then for the *Washington Evening Star* from 1907 until his death in 1949. I've included some of his wonderfully whimsical creations.

"They Won't Agree on Anything" September 24, 1922
As they exit the Capitol and return home to campaign for reelection, the Republican elephant and Democratic donkey have differing perspectives on the session. The elephant remembers Republican successes while the donkey remembers the Republican majority's failures; each hopes this leads to their party's victory in the upcoming election.
Clifford Berryman, U.S. Senate Collection Center for Legislative Archives

"How His Voice Has Changed!" March 4, 1920
Before the 1920 Presidential election, perennial candidate William Jennings Bryan announced he did not desire the Democratic Presidential nomination. But, as a three-time party nominee with two additional attempts seeking his party's nomination, his announcement was received with skepticism. An old-fashioned record player, known as a Victrola, spreads his message. The Democrats nominated James M. Cox, Governor of Ohio, who lost the Presidential election to Republican Warren G. Harding.
Clifford Berryman, U.S. Senate Collection Center for Legislative Archives

"The Fishin' Season" June 7, 1919
When this cartoon was published the 1920 Presidential election was nearly a year and a half away. There were no clear front-runners and both major parties were in need of a campaign platform that would lead their party to victory. The cartoon captures the Republican elephant and the Democratic donkey seated on the same log fishing on different sides of the "campaign issues pool."
Clifford Berryman, U.S. Senate Collection Center for Legislative Archives

"*Nearing the End of the Primaries*" *May 3, 1920*
Today candidates usually secure their party's nomination during the primary season, and the nominating convention merely provides the party's official stamp of approval. In 1920, however, when the primary process was still new, it did not produce a clear winner for the Republican Party. As the Republican convention neared, there was no front-runner for the G.O.P. Presidential nomination. This cartoon shows the frazzled Republican elephant surrounded by conflicting newspaper headlines while the Democratic donkey makes pressing inquiries. Warren G. Harding was eventually chosen as the Republican nominee.
Clifford Berryman, U.S. Senate Collection Center for Legislative Archives

"Democratic New Years Eve Cheer" December 31, 1931
In the 1930 congressional elections, Republicans retained a slim majority in both houses of
Congress. When the new Congress convened in December 1931, however, a number of deaths
and departures left vacancies in seats held by Republicans. Results from special elections held
to fill these seats shifted control of the House of Representatives to the Democrats. The Demo-
cratic donkey, cheered by his party's new power, consoles the defeated Republican elephant as
the old year sets over the horizon.
Clifford Berryman, U.S. Senate Collection Center for Legislative Archives

CHAPTER 8

LET'S HAVE A VOTER RALLY

It's not the hand that signs the laws that holds the destiny of America. It's the hand that casts the ballot.
Harry S. Truman

I n the world of Your Vote Is Magic! there were so many balls in the air at this time, and every ball depended on the next one to fall correctly into place. I couldn't sit idle for three weeks until I met the new zoo director, so I began thinking of other important details. I wanted the event to be filmed so I could use the footage to further promote the message. (This, in turn, has led to the writing of this book.) I know how to make magic happen, but coming up with all the components around the illusion was something I felt unsure about. So I hired marketing engineer Ron Fortier.

With Ron on board, we quickly developed the concept of having a voter rally as the prelude to the illusion. It would be complete with a town hall meeting centered on voting; speakers, including politicians; patriotic music; and, of course, voter registration. I thought calling it Your Vote Is Magic! would be perfect for the theme, especially since every person's vote is truly magic, and that is the reason for all of this happening. We were both pretty confident at the time that the money could be raised to cover the costs.

Finally it was time to run the idea by the new zoo director, Dr. William Langbauer. We hoped his interest in elephants would help out my cause. Again, a lot was riding on his decision. If he wasn't behind the idea or thought it would be too much for the Zoo to handle, then I had zero chance of doing it at the Buttonwood Park Zoo. Another deep breath.

Of course, he shared the same collective concern as the zoo-keepers, but he thought it would be a great way to get people's attention with the message and was totally behind it! Whew! Now he had to clear it all with Mayor Lang to make sure they were both on the same page with the project. Finally, after a few more weeks, I received the green light to proceed.

CHAPTER 9

OH, TO BE POLITICALLY CORRECT

Always vote for principle, though you may vote alone, and you may cherish the sweetest reflection that your vote is never lost.
John Quincy Adams

One day in the early spring, Abner, the donkey, and Judy came down to the Zoo for a brief afternoon visit. We needed to make sure that Abner and Emily wouldn't totally freak out around each other. Once again, it felt like we were sitting on the edge of our seats. Would either animal be so uncomfortable that Abner couldn't represent the Democratic Party in the illusion?

I also wanted some of the head animal keepers to meet Abner. A horse trailer and driver had to be rented for his transportation. When he arrived, he didn't want to get out of the trailer. Understandably, Abner was very nervous. But with a lot of prodding and treats, he finally stepped out. He wasn't too close to Emily, but at least they were both okay and the animal keepers loved him! They had given Abner some hay to walk on and eat. The keepers wanted his scent on the hay to place in Emily's den after he left so she could adjust to his scent. He passed the test with everyone but, of course, his owner, Judy, was with him and it was a very elementary introduction. However, we all felt confident that we had conquered another hurdle. It was also very important that Judy felt comfortable that Abner would be in a safe environment and in the capable, experienced care of the animal handlers. Fortunately, she was quite impressed with the zoo and the team who would be working with him.

The timing of Abner's arrival was in question because

the Zoo would be going through its accreditation process . . . a very stressful ordeal for the entire Zoo staff. The AZA (American Zoological Association) spends a few days at the Zoo, and its staff goes through every exhibit with a fine-tooth comb to ensure the Zoo is up to its standards. Everyone at the Zoo is extremely busy preparing for their visit. We figured it would be mid-summer before Abner could come. Hmmm, would that be enough time? The date for the event and illusion was September 13. It would be a little tight, but should be doable, I thought, if we start having Abner do some pre-training procedures with Judy.

I also realized, with the importance of the illusion being non-partisan, that it dictated both animals having to appear at the same time. Originally, I thought I'd produce the donkey and repeat the illusion and have the elephant appear. But no matter who appeared first, there might have been some political fallout and I couldn't take the risk. That's certainly not what the message was about. Hmmm, both animals at the same time would be even more dicey, because as they were being produced, they would have to calmly stand next to each other while the framework came down around them. But whoever said this was going to be easy!

I had to run that idea by the trainers. They were also concerned, but all agreed it was the politically correct way to present the illusion. It would just take longer to work with Emily and Abner to ensure there would be no problems.

Abner's owner, Judy, coaxing him over to meet Emily on his first visit to the Zoo. Kay Santos, one of the elephant keepers is to Judy's left and Shelley Avila-Martins is to her right. Emily, the elephant is pictured on the right and Ruth is on the left.

Abner, a large standard donkey, will represent the mascot of the Democratic Party in the illusion..

For the illusion, Emily, an Asian elephant, will represent the mascot of the Republican Party.

CHAPTER 10

FORGING AHEAD

I always decide my vote by taking as careful a look as I can at the actual candidates and issues themselves, no matter what the party label.

Jackie Robinson

n June of '08, Ron had arranged a press conference at the Zoo so we could publicly announce Your Vote Is Magic!. On that morning, my mother had become very ill from the lung disease she has and was rushed to the hospital because she could hardly breathe. The Emergency Room doctors weren't sure if she had a pulmonary embolism. She was so upset about me missing the press conference that it made her blood pressure spike. She pleaded with me to go to the Zoo. I didn't want to leave her, but I knew that for the next few hours, while waiting for the results, I couldn't do anything to help her and she might feel better if I went to the Zoo. I raced home, got changed and raced to the Zoo with minutes to spare.

All I could think of was my mother and I just kept praying she'd be okay. Nothing else mattered at that point except her health. The press conference seemed like a blur. Gosh, was this a sign of how the project was going to go? Thankfully, she came home later that day and just needed some time to recuperate from an exacerbation of her condition. What a huge relief!

During the month of June, Judy shipped Abner up to Vermont to get a head start with the training process. Kris Anderson, an accomplished, professional handler, worked wonders with him. She used clicker training and would take a video of him and post it on YouTube so I could watch it and see his progress. Once he got back to Judy's he continued his training, and every day he listened to a CD that I had made. It had everything from elephants trumpeting to crowd noises to fireworks—anything that could potentially spook him. The key with the training was to desensitize the animals. Every single element of the illusion had to be thought through for the safety of the trainers, animals, my crew, and the crowd. Emily, who weighed almost 8,000 pounds, was a "big girl," and if anything frightened her it could cause a chain reaction of movement and someone could get seriously hurt. We knew, during the rehearsals, that we would have to create as many potential scenarios as possible so the animals would be totally prepared.

I started to work on the engineering and set-design of the illusion. My crew and I met with a production team to discuss some of the technical aspects of the structure. It would take six hundred feet of truss and over one hundred lighting units. It was technically much more intricate than the cruder version of the illusion I had performed eight years earlier. Aside from the engineering concerns, I had to decide where on the Zoo's grounds the illusion would take place. I visited the Zoo countless times and brought tape measures and rope to mark out exactly where the footprint of the illusion would be. It had to be as precise as possible so the production team would know where to set up the massive structure.

The site that Lyn chose on the Zoo's premises for the illusion.

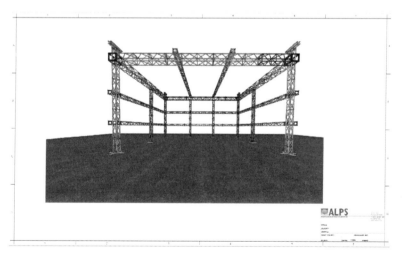

CAD (Computer aided drawing) of the illusion.

Next on the agenda was to start the rehearsal process. As I mentioned, I had worked with the Buttonwood Park Zoo's resident elephants, Emily and Ruth, eight years ago. For this new illusion, only Emily would be used. We had to shower Ruth with lots of attention so she wouldn't feel left out. That was a cinch to do since everyone just melts when they are around Ruth. I had to have the framework that was manufactured for the illusion brought into the elephant barn and rigged up with an electric hoist. This would enable the animal trainers to press a button and have this 18-foot by 14-foot aluminum frame, with practice fabric attached to it, lowered around Emily. She needed to get used to the motion of the frame and comfortable with her boundaries standing inside of it, as it lowered to the ground. It took a whole day just to rig it up. The entire frame had to be pulled up about twenty feet in the air so Emily and Ruth couldn't tamper with it.

As part of the illusion when the animals appeared, I wanted Emily to hold onto an American flag. Well, you know that old saying that an elephant never forgets? It's very true! When I saw Emily practicing with the frame, she was as excited as she was eight years ago when she did it. Emily squealed as her ears were flapping and tail was wagging while waving the flag in her trunk! She was absolutely adorable! The zookeepers and I were laughing hysterically. Working with Emily was like working with a dear, old friend.

There were times during some of the rehearsals with other elements of the illusion when Emily was a little insecure, so the trainers would bring Ruth over first and have her investigate. When she started playing with the props, it made Emily want to play too. Ruth diffused any apprehension Emily had. As Jenny explains, "We used the elephants' natural social structure in their behavior to facilitate Emily's acclimation to the props we were using. Then we paired it all with positive reinforcement and constantly gave her all the positive reinforcement she could stand."

It was such a simple, but brilliant training strategy. How the trainers dealt with every aspect of the training process constantly impressed and amazed me. Their instincts were always spot-on. For example, as far as knowing how long to work with Emily on one of her tasks, Jenny explained their philosophy: "When we got something spectacular out of her, like the first time we were able to drop the frame around Emily, we did it once and she got jackpotted, and then she didn't have to do it again that day. Soon after, she started coming back and wanting to do more and play with it more, so we were able to extend our training sessions. We always left on a good note. If Emily was unsure, we'd always find something positive to end on."

Since performing the original illusion with Emily and Ruth back in 2000, I've been very fortunate to be able to maintain my very special friendship with them. Every so often, I visit them at the Zoo and bring them treats. I am still in awe of them when I am around them. There really is something very magical about both of them, individually and certainly when they are together. They are just incredible animals and I love them both dearly.

A smaller, lighter frame made from PVC (polyvinyl chloride) with tarps attached was erected in a barn for Abner to practice with when he arrived. Able to move up and down with ropes and pulleys, it was a much cruder version of the actual frame for the illusion in the elephant barn, but it did the trick (no pun intended). Finally, in mid-July he was able to come down to the Zoo.

Now there were some new speed bumps to contend with. There was a quarantine issue with Abner. He would have to be isolated from all the animals, including Emily, for thirty days. Originally, it was going to be two weeks. The Zoo's veterinarian found out that the protocol required four weeks. This meant that Abner wouldn't be able to get close to Emily for an entire month. And after that, we would only have two weeks to get Abner and Emily used to being side by side before the actual illusion rehearsals that would last another two weeks. This was starting to become a nail biter!

Lyn with her pal Emily

CHAPTER 11

PROMOTING THE IDEA

I never vote for anyone. I always vote against.
W. C. Fields

n the next few weeks, Ron and I met with Comcast to help
with the public service campaign. They gave us 1,200 public service advertisements to air on television to promote the
Your Vote Is Magic! voting message. The ads were so much fun
to produce. In keeping with the magic theme, I tore up a voting ballot and restored it to an American flag with the message
being "Freedom Is Not An Illusion, VOTE!" The other ad featured my rabbit, Bixby, who was used in my show sitting on top
of a ballot box and then starting to multiply on the screen—
hence the "Multiply Your Vote" theme. We also received in-
kind sponsorship from a prominent local radio station, WBSM
AM 1420. I started to do a lot of talk radio shows to create
some interest and excitement about the project. There were
many times when people would call in live and be very passionate about their views on voting. Just about every caller was
very supportive of the idea of people taking voting seriously,
getting involved, and registering to vote if they weren't regis-
tered already. All of the callers were in agreement that maybe
their candidate of choice wouldn't get elected, but if they didn't
engage in the voting process then he or she had no chance; and
if they didn't vote at all, then they would have no right to complain about what's wrong in our country. I started to realize that
I had quite a responsibility to pull this off successfully, because
I had the potential to really make an impact with this message.
I felt a definite weight on my shoulders. It was a good weight,

though. People were putting their faith and trust in me that this would be a worthwhile cause. It was very inspiring!

A challenge that Ron and I ran into was keeping the actual illusion under wraps. I needed to tease the public about it but not reveal what would happen, because the element of surprise is essential and I wanted the audience to be blown away. If they knew what to expect, it would be like knowing a comedian's punch line before he or she delivers it. The whole climax is diluted and it lessens the impact.

Ken Pittman, a prominent local radio host from WBSM, was hugely supportive of Your Vote Is Magic! and kept plugging the event. He offered to co-host the event with a live remote. Ken leans to the right politically (Republican) and we needed a co-host who leaned to the left (Democrat). He knew Ellen Ratner, who is a very well-respected political analyst from Fox National News and the Network Bureau Chief for Talk Radio News. Ellen would call in to the radio station every day from Washington with the current political news. Ken had invited her to co-host the event. We waited weeks for her reply. Finally, one afternoon when I was listening to Ken talking to Ellen on-air, she accepted our invitation. This was a big plus for the event. Ellen had quite a local following in the area and she was a national name. I was psyched and very honored!

"Your Vote Is Magic" posters designed by Lyn's marketing engineer, Ron Fortier

Freedom ★ Is Not An Illusion...

VOTE

Voter Information & Registration Event!
Buttonwood Park Zoo
Saturday, September 13 from 6:30 to 9
FOOD – SPEAKERS – MAGIC

Ken Pittman

WBSM Personality - Moderating the Town Hall Style Meeting

YOUR VOTE IS MAGIC!
Voter Information
& Registration Event

This message brought to you by in-part by
The Educational, Economic and Cultural Resource
The Weekly Compass

You Don't Have to Be a Magician to Create Change...

VOTE

Voter Information & Registration Event!
Buttonwood Park Zoo
Saturday, September 13 from 6:30 to 9
FOOD – SPEAKERS · MAGIC

YOUR VOTE IS MAGIC!
Voter Information
& Registration Event

This message brought to you by in-part by...

Office of the Mayor
City of New Bedford

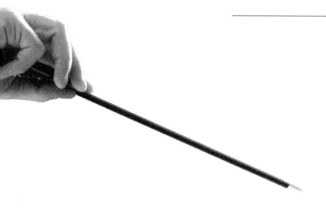

CHAPTER 12

LOTS TO DO

The politicians were talking themselves red, white and blue in the face.
Claire Booth Luce

started contacting politicians to ask them to be part of the speaker agenda for the actual event. I invited them to talk to the crowd about the importance of voting and why this election year would impact all of us. I reached out to some very prominent politicians. The one who I kept dreaming about attending was the (late) Senator Ted Kennedy. I had invited him to be the keynote speaker. His staff said that because of health issues it would be impossible for him to make that commitment. His brain tumor had been diagnosed earlier that year. I truly felt that if he hadn't been ill he would have been there. He was very fond of the New Bedford area and was such a champion of worthwhile causes. Some of the legwork required a few trips to the statehouse in Boston to touch base with some congressmen, as well as sending out letters and e-mails and lots of follow-up phone calls. I was so touched when Senator Michael Rodrigues told me he would be honored to be a speaker. He could certainly talk from experience about every person's vote counting. After speaking with him I learned quite a bit more about his first election experience. It reinforced everything my father taught me about voting. Senator Rodrigues recalled that when he ran for state representative, it was his first time running for public office. Prior to his first run, his public service only involved appointed positions.

At the time, the state representative seat was a very hotly

contested one. It had been held by the very popular Ed Lambert, who was then running for mayor. Six people were in the race. Senator Rodrigues spoke about how tense the evening was. He explained to me that back then some of his committee members would be at the Registrar of Voters office and call in the votes from the various precincts, which would be written on a chalkboard. He was behind 56 votes in the last precinct. He and his committee were just waiting for the final results.

I asked him if, at that point in the evening, he had a victory or concession speech prepared. He said, "I had neither one prepared. I was just going to speak from the heart." Well, the final tally came into the precinct and Mike had won by seven votes! They did have a recount and he mentioned that my father was present for it. He reflected back and remembered how happy he was to be able to give a victory speech, but also thought of the individual who lost by seven votes. "I think of him as he looks over the voter list and saw who didn't vote. How you vote is private, it's between you and God. But if you vote, whether or not you voted is public record. So how many of his friends, family, neighbors and supporters did not go to vote? I'm sure he could identify at least eight which would have made him the victor." Whenever Senator Rodrigues can, he reaches out to high school students to convince them that their vote really matters.

I asked him what was perhaps most memorable about my father's involvement in his campaign. It was so great to talk with him about my dad because it was such a direct, personal connection about my father's passion for politics and for making a difference. He told me that my father was like an advisor who had common-sense advice and told it like it was. As Mike recalled, "As you run for elected office, you get a lot of pats on the back and most people tell you what you want to hear. But your father was one of my real friends, who wouldn't be afraid to say, 'Mike, what's wrong with you? Why are you saying that? I disagree with your position on this issue . . . are you sure you want to do that?' And when it's campaign time, those are the people you want around you. And even if you lose, they will still be your friends."

He remembered my father telling him, "Never forget where you came from." Mike explained that it was really good advice and he repeats it to himself all the time because "It's really easy to get lost in the statehouse. I see it happen to people all the time when they get there. It's an exciting place to work. You're working on very dynamic, important issues. Even for people who are very hard-working and well-meaning, it's easy to get lost up there. You're doing the work you wanted to do when you were elected to office, like affecting change, having the opportunity to amend or modify laws to make things better for people. But never forget where you came from. You have to stay connected to your constituency. If you want to stay in office you have to remember that no one in the statehouse votes for you. Everyone who's going to put you back in office is back home, wherever that home may be. So your father's advice was to just never forget where you came from. He'd say, 'You're a Westporter, Mike, you're a working guy, you come from a blue collar family.' I'll never forget that."

CHAPTER 13

YOUR VOTE COUNTS... AND RECOUNTS

The first lesson is this: take it from me, every vote counts.
Al Gore

As demonstrated by Senator Rodrigues, every vote certainly does matter. Some people think there's no point in voting because their one little vote will be a drop in the bucket. Well, all of those little drops add up to a very big bucket and determine who the winner is. And as you will read, sometimes in a very close election a recount is needed. Just in case you're not convinced how much your vote counts, take a look at some of these fascinating examples:

1941: The Selective Service Act (the draft) was saved by a one-vote margin in the House of Representatives just weeks before the attack on Pearl Harbor.

1948: In a primary for one of Texas's two senate seats, Lyndon Johnson earned the ironic nickname "Landslide Lyndon" for squeezing out an 87-vote victory.

1948: The Presidential Race: Dewey vs. Truman: Harry Truman was a significant underdog in the race for president. Yet he narrowly defeated republican Thomas Dewey by winning Ohio and California to secure the electoral college. Harry Truman also won the popular vote. This tremendous upset created one of the most famous, and incorrect, newspaper headlines of all-time, "Dewey Defeats Truman."

1984: Rep. Frank McCloskey (D-Ind.): After a controversial recount, he was reelected by a mere four votes.

1993: In New Bedford, Massachusetts, Cynthia Kruger

ran against George Smith for ward councilor of a city district. After a recount, Cynthia Kruger won by three votes.

2000: The presidential race between Al Gore and George W. Bush was a bit of an illusion! Before millions of Americans went to bed that night, the news media mistakenly reported that Al Gore had won. Americans were quite surprised to learn the next morning that George W. Bush had been declared the winner. The election was so close that each party became embroiled in a controversy. The state in question was Florida and, coincidentally, Jeb Bush, George W. Bush's younger brother, was Florida's governor. The difference in votes was only 537 out of 5.9 million cast. It was an unprecedented election and the U.S. Supreme Court decided to stop the recount before it was finished. Al Gore conceded and George W. Bush was elected president.

2002: Former Rep. Bob Beauprez (R-Colo.) defeated his democratic opponent and won by 121 votes.

2004: State of Washington gubernatorial race, Gregoire vs. Rossi: Democrat Christine O'Grady Gregoire defeated Republican Dino Rossi by 133 votes out of 2.8 million cast. The result was finalized after multiple recounts and lawsuits. In 2008 Rossi challenged Gregoire again and this time was defeated more decisively.

2008: Minnesota Senate Race, Franken vs. Coleman: In the race for one of Minnesota's senate seats, Al Franken defeated incumbent republican Norm Coleman by 312 votes. More than 2.4 million votes were cast in the election. Al Franken emerged victorious after Coleman challenged the results in court. The Minnesota Supreme Court ruled in favor of Franken.

January 3, 2012: Former Governor Mitt Romney won by a razor-thin margin in the Iowa caucuses, beating former Pennsylvania Senator Rick Santorum by just eight votes. The final tally was 30,015 votes for Romney and 30,007 votes for Santorum.

Finally, every election is important, no matter how small.

April 11, 2012: In Rochester, Massachusetts, a park commission contest was held for a seat on the board. Kenneth Ross won the race against incumbent Travis Lalli by one vote. The vote count was 120 to 119. It doesn't get any closer than that![2]

CHAPTER 14

WHAT IT TOOK

There can no longer be anyone too poor to vote.
Lyndon B. Johnson

Preparations for the event continued. Not surprisingly, I ran into some more snags, like finding out that insurance certificates and bonds had to be taken out, and special permits were needed from the City of New Bedford and the Buttonwood Park Board. Even one thing going wrong would totally put an end to my dream becoming a reality. One night, Ron and I made a presentation to the Buttonwood Park Board so they could vote to grant me permission to hold the event on the park grounds. Of course, some members joked about me being able to make certain politicians disappear. They all gave us a big "thumbs up" and were very supportive and enthusiastic. Every day was chock-a-block full of appointments, phone calls, e-mails and, of course, numerous trips to the Zoo.

Through the entire journey, I always felt like my father was guiding me. We met so many politicians together, and attended many fundraisers and campaign events. Some of the Your Vote Is Magic! process felt like second nature. Many people remembered him so fondly, and that gave me more motivation and strength to keep going. Every time I started to get consumed with the project, my father was my compass getting me back on track. And what this whole endeavor boiled down to was what Americans would be doing on November 4th.

It's amazing to think of what we take for granted when

we go to vote. Most of us mull over our decision for weeks or months, deciding which candidate is best for the job. And it isn't made easier by the barrage of television commercials we are exposed to as election day nears, each presenting differing points of view, depending upon the party affiliation. Finally, we go to the polls. But what it took for us to be able to walk into a school or town hall and cast our vote is certainly worth learning about. It wasn't easy!

When America was founded, the right to vote was not written into the U.S. Constitution. Each state had its own standards for voting until federal laws were passed to universally allow voting in every state. During early American history, only white men who owned property could vote in every state, but freed slaves of African descent could vote in just four states, and some women were allowed to vote in a few western states. White working men, almost all women and all other people of color were denied the right to vote. Due to the tireless work of those who believed in suffrage, most white men, whether they were property owners or not, were allowed to vote by the time of the Civil War. Then as now, one had to be a U.S. citizen to qualify for the right to vote; but at that time, many minorities, including American Indians, Mexican-Americans, Central and South Americans, and Asians, were not citizens yet.

In 1848, in Seneca Falls, New York, a group of women

formed the Women's Suffrage Movement, to organize efforts to allow women to vote.

In 1869, after the American Civil War, the Fifteenth Amendment to the Constitution was passed, allowing black men to vote. Even though the Fifteenth Amendment granted black men their voting rights, it was corrupted. How? That same year, "Black Codes" were formed, which restricted many freedoms of African Americans. It "appeared" that they had the full right to vote, but in fact, that right was hindered by state laws that precluded them from voting. Poll taxes, literacy tests, even secret poll locations were all ways to keep the African Americans from voting, mostly in the southern states. In the Southwest, Latinos were facing many of the same issues.

In observing a small legislative step forward and what seemed to be two steps backward, there was still the fact that women were excluded from equal voting rights. The women heading up the movement for women's suffrage, Susan B. Anthony and Elizabeth Cady Stanton, felt the Fifteenth Amendment was inadequate. Lucy Stone and Julia Ward Howe thought it would eventually lead to women voting. As a result, two new organizations were created: The National Woman Suffrage Association and the American Woman Suffrage Association. They later merged into the National American Woman Suffrage Association (NAWSA) headed by Stanton, Stone and Anthony.

Susan B. Anthony and Elizabeth Cady Stanton - two of the most prominent activists in the Women's Suffrage movement

In 1913, two NAWSA members, Alice Paul and Lucy Burns, formed different views about its strategy and founded the Congressional Union, which became the National Woman's Party (NWP). The NWP adopted a more militant approach to gaining women's rights.

A long road lay ahead in the national struggle for equal voting rights. History reveals that lives were lost, brutality was widespread and condoned, and the path to voting equality was unthinkably difficult. Heroes and heroines emerged all along the way.

Let's focus on the women's suffrage movement as a painful look back before ultimate triumph.

On February 19, 2004, Connie Schultz from *The Plain Dealer* reported the following story: It was spring of 1917. Woodrow Wilson had been re-elected to his second term and the United States had declared war on Germany. The new National Woman's Party started to picket outside of the White House and the Capitol. Slowly, the untraditional, impassioned way the members of the NWP were campaigning began gaining national attention. They seemed to stop at nothing, despite knowing the very real risk of being arrested and going to jail.

And arrests came. In the first round of arrests, women were sentenced to spend three days in a district jail that at least had running water and bath facilities. Subsequent ar-

Suffragists parade down Fifth Avenue, in October 1917, displaying placards containing the signatures of more than one million New York women demanding the vote.
The New York Times Photo Archives

Woman suffragists picketing outside the White House when President Woodrow Wilson held office. Library of Congress

More picketers protesting against President Woodrow Wilson's lack of support for Women's Suffrage. Library of Congress

rests carried the same penalty.

On July 14, 1917, all that changed. Despite the arrests, momentum continued to build along with the picketing demonstrations. And now these women were viewed as being unpatriotic and disrespectful to President Wilson. Thirty-three women were arrested and sentenced to sixty days at an abandoned workhouse located in Lorton, Virginia. The warden of the Occoquan Workhouse, W. H. Whittaker, ordered his guards to use brutal force against the women suffragists, to punish them for having the audacity to picket the White House.

Nothing could have prepared the women for how violently they would be treated. Some were literally thrown into their cells and became seriously injured. One prisoner suffered a heart attack; another ended up unconscious, the result of hitting her head against a metal bed after being hurled into her cell.

The conditions at the Occoquan Workhouse were deplorable and inhumane. The cells were cold and overrun with rats. The water and food provided were unsanitary. An affidavit from one of the prison guards described the food served to the prisoners as being worm-infested.

National Association Headquarters Opposed to Women's Suffrage.
Library of Congress

Alice Paul, another prisoner, and one of the suffragist leaders, decided she would protest the wretched conditions by going on a hunger strike. The guards didn't want her to become a symbol of the cause, so they force-fed her by inserting a tube down her throat. After weeks of suffering the unimaginable, word of their torture got out to the press and to the public. Thus, they finally gained the compassion and respect that they needed to help their cause.

It took an intense seventy two-year coordinated movement for women to gain suffrage, during which

Alice Paul, head of the National Woman's Party, was often arrested and imprisoned. Library of Congress

time thousands of women survived mob attacks, physical beatings and rapes. They continued to protest, organize marches, petition and lobby, and in 1920 they won! The passage of the Nineteenth Amendment to the Constitution gave women the right to vote.

In 1965, after one-hundred years of denying the privilege of voting to many groups, President Lyndon B. Johnson was largely responsible for the passage of the Voting Rights

Dora Lewis of Philadelphia, released after a five-day hunger strike in prison. Too ill to walk on her own, she is being physically helped by fellow suffragists Clara Louise Rowe (left) and Abby Scott Baker (right).
Library of Congress

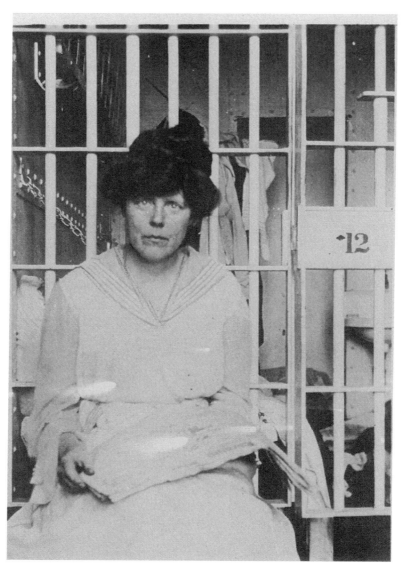

Lucy Burns in Occoquan Workhouse in November, 1917. She served more time in jail than any other suffragist. Library of Congress

Mrs. Helena Hill Weed: a well-known woman suffragist jailed in Occoquan Workhouse. At the time of her death in 1958, she was hailed by TIME Magazine as a "kinetic suffragette who crisscrossed the nation crusading for the right to vote." Library of Congress

The Nineteenth Amendment: Women casting their votes in New York City, c. 1920. Library of Congress

Act (VRA). It finally prohibited racial discrimination and eliminated poll taxes and literary tests. All that was required to vote anywhere in the country was U.S. citizenship and registration on an electoral list. The VRA is probably one of the most legendary pieces of legislation in U.S. Government, and possibly one of President Johnson's greatest accomplishments. Here's part of the memorable speech he made to Congress to get the Voting Rights Act passed:

"Rarely are we met with a challenge...to the values and the purposes and the meaning of our beloved Nation. The issue of equal rights for American Negroes is such as an issue... the command of the Constitution is plain. It is wrong - deadly wrong - to deny any of your fellow Americans the right to vote in this country."

Another important legislative milestone happened in June of 1971. The voting age was lowered to age 18, which allowed 11.5 million young Americans to vote in all state, local and national elections.

It's sobering to think of what Americans – men and women of all nationalities – endured through history in order to be able to vote. It is the hard-won privilege of having a say, to matter as a citizen, to be given the power to influence government policies that affect every aspect of our lives. It's astonishing to think of what it took throughout our history to allow this basic freedom. And all the more sad to think that some actually take it for granted.[3]

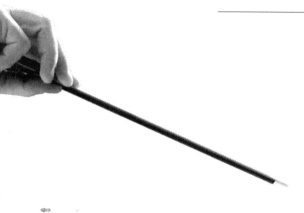

CHAPTER 15

ABNER'S ESCAPADES

Those who have long enjoyed such privileges as we enjoy forget in time that men have died to win them.
Franklin D. Roosevelt

Sarah, who was Abner's trainer, immediately connected with Abner. A few days after his arrival, Sarah was kicked in her elbow by one of the draft horses at the Zoo. Thankfully she was okay but was out of work almost a week with a bad contusion. Okay Lyn, don't panic! Soon Sarah came back and was ready to start working with Abner. Even though Abner couldn't get near Emily, he could see and smell Emily from a distance. We found that Abner's favorite treats for clicker training were peanut butter-filled pretzels. Emily loved red seedless grapes. While practicing with Emily, we'd have to make sure her companion, Ruth, had grapes as well, so she wouldn't feel left out. One of our sponsors, Lee's Supermarket from Westport, provided at least eighteen pounds of grapes per week. That's a lot of grapes! Every time I went to Lee's Supermarket to pick up the boxes of grapes, the customers must have thought I must really love red seedless grapes!

I checked in on Abner each day to make sure he was okay. I had a feeling that on one particular day Sarah was going to start working with him. As I approached his enclosure, I saw Sarah giving him some treats. She came over to me and looked startled. She said that when she took Abner down the path to where the elephants are located, he pretty much dragged her about thirty feet in his halter while she was holding onto him for dear life. Not a good sign. As Sarah recalled, "For the first week-and-a-half being away from his owner, Judy, he was very difficult to work with. I couldn't get him to walk on a lead and I couldn't get him to listen. He was being a donkey. He wasn't used to us and we weren't used to him. It took a little give-and-take to get the relationship to work, and once we got over that hump it was a lot smoother."

Judy also drove down to reassure Sarah that she could handle him. She needed to feel that it was okay to take control. Luckily, after a few more days, Abner realized that Sarah was the boss and started to cooperate much better. Sarah, Jenny and Kay started easing Abner into the frame to get used to it lowering around him. They would walk him over the frame when it was down on the ground, and then place him in the middle of it and bring up the curtain around him and slowly lower it. He did bolt a couple of times but they kept at it. Sarah did a lot of walking with Abner back and forth to the elephant barn during the day. Despite all of the challenges, Abner and Sarah developed quite a special bond. I was already dreading the day Sarah would have to say goodbye to Abner.

During one of my visits, I heard this really strange sound. It sounded like it was coming from Abner's direction. Well, guess what? It was Abner! For whatever reason, he started to bray. It's the typical cry that a donkey makes but we never thought he brayed. Judy never heard him bray and thought he was typically pretty silent. It certainly surprised all of us, and especially Judy when I phoned her. Just another worry to add to the list. Suppose Abner decided to bray before he was magically produced!

Judy Ballantine, Abner's owner, having a chat with him at the Buttonwood Park Zoo.

Lyn with Abner, on one of her visits to check on him.

Abner still wasn't too happy about the practice frame lowering around him. At least he and Sarah were much more comfortable with each other. It took a lot of coordination among the trainers just to rehearse it. Every time Sarah would work with Abner, Kay would help as well. Since Abner's practice barn was near Emily and Ruth's barn, two keepers had to be around Emily to make sure she wasn't rattled if she saw Abner. They tried to practice with Abner and the frame about twice a day. Everyone had to be on the same page. It was sometimes difficult to get all of the keepers needed for the training together during the day because they had their regular duties at the Zoo to tend to. It was becoming very stressful for everyone. We all felt the clock ticking. At this point, the whole project was still a big IF.

In order for this to have any chance of being a success, I had to keep on going every day under the premise that it would all work out. Talk about taking chances! I wouldn't know until maybe one or two weeks before the event if this would truly work. Whenever I had any doubts about Your Vote Is Magic!, whenever I wondered if I had gotten in over my head, whenever I questioned my instincts about the concept, whenever I was too exhausted to think straight, I would focus on my father's memory and how proud he would be of it all. He was the strength I drew from, along with my mother's constant love and support.

Finally, when the quarantine ended, we got Abner and Emily a little closer to each other every day. It was going quite well. Jenny recalled one of the funniest moments during our journey. "The whole time the trainers were together, we kept saying, 'Emily's fine with Abner until she's not.' And we didn't want to see what would happen when she stopped being fine, which is why we didn't let Emily have any direct contact with him. We didn't want to push it. She was doing fine. It was the second or third day we had them together without a boundary (no barrier between them), and they were standing in the positions that they were going to be in when they'd be revealed for the illusion. And so it was Sarah, Abner, me and Emily. And we were all talking about how great they were doing and how steady they were. All of a sudden, Abner sneezed and Emily jumped—probably three feet straight up in the air and over about a foot-and-a-half away from Abner. She grabbed my arm with her trunk and was like, "What was that?!!!" And then she turned to face Abner and pushed her ears out and forward to listen closely and make herself look bigger. She started squeaking as if to say, "You just made a wicked, weird noise there, what happened?" It was a riot, and we were all collapsing in laughter, but it was sobering to realize the potential danger. We immediately got them close to each other again and everything was okay. We always had to end each training session on a positive note, so that's what they would remember.

And as Shara remembered about the training process, "We knew we had to push the envelope but there were so many 'what if's.' What if X happens or Y happens? How are we going to be prepared for it? You're dealing with a 7,800-pound animal, and if she panics she could cause a world of damage."

CHAPTER 16

DETAILS, DETAILS...

The ignorance of one voter in a democracy impairs the security of all.
John F. Kennedy

While the daily training process was happening, there were countless details and tasks to tend to, including getting out publicity for the event; lining up live patriotic music; distributing postcards and flyers; going for costume fittings; arranging food vendors; and, believe it or not, figuring out how many port-a-johns to rent. There were lots of meetings with city officials about staging needed for the rally, electrical requirements for the film crew, and issues related to food vendors and the sound system for the illusion and rally, among many others.

I met with the New Bedford Election Commissioner, Maria Tomasia, a number of times to discuss various ways to publicize the event. She gathered her own team of volunteers to do some guerilla marketing for the event. At least 5,000 flyers and postcards were distributed. Maria was always so enthusiastic and supportive about Your Vote Is Magic! It was an election commissioner's dream!

One of the things I looked most forward to was getting to work with my music composer, Joe Carrier, on the score for the illusion. He's an absolute genius and nailed the composition. It definitely gave me goosebumps the first time I heard the piece. It had the triumphant and patriotic feel I was hoping for. He also donated some of his time, which was hugely appreciated. This endeavor was certainly going to cost a significant amount of money.

I contacted my good friend Dave Lebeau, who owns Lightworks Productions, the largest sound and lighting company in the Southcoast, about renting the sound equipment and some of the lighting equipment for the entire event. Dave had been technical director for my show for a few years. He really believed in the message of Your Vote Is Magic! I was so touched when he told me he wanted to donate all of the equipment needed for the event. He was there every night of the rehearsals lending his time and talent. His contribution to the cause was HUGE!

Next on my checklist was to coordinate a team of volunteers for the illusion. Besides my own crew who work for my show, I needed about 10 volunteers just to help with the illusion--and that didn't include the people needed for the rally and other tasks. We had enough interest but the challenge for most was to be available on a consistent basis for twelve nights in a row. And we couldn't have any stand-ins because once someone was trained, we didn't have the time to retrain that person at the last minute. Everyone had their own special, unique job. Fortunately, we were able to line up some wonderful volunteers who were very dedicated to our endeavor.

I had the illusion to be concerned about as well as organizing the voter rally and many other details. The execution of the illusion was by far the biggest priority. But every day I'd contact businesses, organizations, and political groups to try to either raise some funds and sponsorships or invite them to be involved in the trade show portion of the event. Everyone loved the concept, thought it was a fantastic, much needed idea; but most businesses or groups had either already allocated monies for sponsorships or donations for the year or they were involved with their own pet projects. Unfortunately, because of the questionable status of doing the illusion, I couldn't have contacted any of the businesses any earlier in the year. Despite all of the financial rejection, I had to keep moving forward. The economy also had a big impact on any potential sponsors. Nonetheless, I did manage to raise some money, but it was a small amount compared to what was needed. I tried very hard to remain as calm as I could. Despite the stress of the animal training and the financial issues, I had to trust that it would all work out.

Also, I very much wanted our veterans to have a presence at the event. Their sacrifice to this country ensures that we have our freedom and the wonderful privilege to vote. I contacted various veterans groups and met a few veterans who said they would enjoy being honored at the event. Getting to know them reminded me of just how phenomenal these people are.

Thinking about what they have done to preserve our freedom prompted me to think back to 9/11. Before 9/11, I, like many of us, took my freedom for granted, but after that horrific day, I never will again. As with any monumental event that happens in our lives, we always remember where we were at that time and what we were doing. I'll never forget on the morning of 9/11, after the first building was struck, my father came running into the house in total disbelief. We were both glued to the television set for the entire day.

The next day, Dad made flag holders for my mother's car and mine. Ten years later, I still have mine in my car where he left it, though the flag is now very faded. It's a constant re-minder of what that day meant for America and my father's love for this country, and that we should never ever forget.

In keeping with the election theme, I thought it would be a fun addition to Your Vote Is Magic! to make a prediction of who would win the election and by what margin. One of our sponsors was Fall River Ford. They donated a brand new, sparkling 2008 Ford Mustang, to be parked inside of the Zoo. On August 27, I placed a clear tube that contained my nota-rized prediction inside of a padlocked box, which was placed on the console of the Mustang. Fernando Garcia, the owner of Fall River Ford, activated the alarm system on the Mustang. The car would be on display until November 5, the day after the election.

For a few evenings, I met with my film director, John Methia, who would be directing the shoot for the illusion-John is a highly skilled Emmy-winning film director. I was so thrilled he was going to be on my team. We needed to make sure we had a general plan in advance concerning camera angles, lighting, etc. I had to talk him through the illusion, step by step, so he could envision what would be happening. Eventually, he'd do an actual site visit to get a clearer idea of what was needed, and then attend one of the preliminary rehearsals. John needed to rent some equipment and line up his own cameramen for the shoot. But everything would happen in due time. Like every part of Your Vote Is Magic! each segment was a puzzle within the master puzzle. It was so fascinating to see the project come together!

Next on my list was to meet with a sign artist who would hand-paint the front canvas with the words Your Vote Is Magic! We needed to discuss the size of the graphic and how it would look on camera, as well as the actual design.

Large drapes of canvas for the illusion had to be sewn by a company in New York City. The exact dimensions were critical because once the structure was set up, it would be too late to send the drapes back. Their size made them too cumbersome to bring to a local seamstress to have altered. I constantly questioned whether I had made the right decision about the weight of the fabric. I didn't want to add any extra strain to the rigging apparatus by having them be too heavy, but also didn't want the sides of the canvas to act like sails if it was windy. Would they be too heavy or too light? Hopefully, just right!

CHAPTER 17

An Afternoon Learning How Voting Impacts Us

To make democracy work, we must be a nation of participants, not simply observers. One who does not vote has no right to complain.

Louis L' Amour

Driving around town I noticed, at almost every turn within a 20-mile radius, a reminder of some of the reasons why voting matters so much. For example, a new school was being built in our area. Elected officials had to approve the funding for the school and, obviously, we elect those officials by voting. One of the roads I was driving on in town was finally getting repaved. I know that it took many months for the selectman to allocate the money for the project. Once again, they were elected to their job and the local citizens voted them in.

As I was approaching a busy intersection, where my mother was in a car accident many years ago, I thought back to when my father and I made sure a stop sign was installed there to make the intersection safer. My mother was broadsided when a truck ran through the intersection without slowing down. Dad and I got petitions signed, and my father brought them in front of the selectmen at a town meeting. The stop sign was voted through. Every vote certainly mattered that night.

On one of my stops that day, I had to pick up a prescription for my mother at the local pharmacy. She now had to pay for her prescriptions out-of-pocket because she had already used up her prescription allowance for the year. This new plan was a result of a bill that passed a few years earlier. It's especially unfortunate for seniors who are on a very limited income. Some actually have to decide between paying their electric bill or getting their medication. Because we depend upon politicians to do the right thing, it's our job to vote for people who have our best interests at heart.

Now, at the time of this writing, I see they are breaking ground for the new fire station in Westport. Wow, it took a few years to get that passed. Sometimes it just takes the right combination of selectman who listen to the taxpayers. Hmm, but what a difference it makes if he or she gets elected. That means it's crucial to get people engaged enough in the issues to VOTE!

Okay, on to New Bedford to check in on Emily and Abner. As I approach the Zoo and the site of the illusion and voter rally, I start thinking about how many emergency personnel and security we're going to need for the event. I know at least a thousand people will be there, but it's possible there could be lots more. The City of New Bedford had been cutting many policemen and firemen due to a budget crisis. I wondered how this would affect the safety of the city's citizens. It would undoubtedly affect the careers of some of my distant relatives who were and still are firefighters in New Bedford. It would not only put a financial burden on them, but also those on the job could be more at risk with less backup personnel.

Once again, we see an example of how our elected officials have a lot of power, influence and control over our lives.

CHAPTER 18

HOW WE VOTE

Every citizen of this country should be guaranteed that their vote matters, that their vote is counted, and that in the voting booth, their vote has as much weight as that of any CEO, any member of Congress, or any President.
Barbara Boxer

With all of these visual reminders of how voting affects us, I felt like taking some time to explore the various ways that we have voted through history.

Here's what I discovered:

In our age of electronic wonders, it's interesting to try and imagine how some of the very earliest voters managed. The word "ballot" can mean the actual method of voting or the act of voting itself. The word ballot is derived from the Italian word *ballotta*, meaning "little ball."

The following are some examples I found fascinating. I hope you will, too!

We have historic records and actual remnants of chards of pottery, pieces of a shell or pebbles that were used to cast a vote. In ancient Greece, a voter would toss one of the objects into an urn. In the early days in America, corn and beans were occasionally used as ballots. And in the ancient time of the Cherokee Indians, when important issues needed to be decided, each tribe member would bring both a black and a white stone or shell bead to the gathering. A white shell or bead represented a positive vote and a black shell or bead represented a negative vote. Each member would place either a white or black bead into a basket.

And now here is a summary of some of our more "modern" ways to vote.

Paper Ballots:

Through voting history, one of the original, easiest ways to vote involved a paper ballot. The earliest paper ballots were called "party tickets," which had the candidates' names printed from only one party on the ticket. Voters would drop their selection into a ballot box. The paper ballot eventually evolved into a ballot with the names of the various candidates printed on the ballot, and the voter would put a mark in the box next to a favored candidate's name, and then drop the ballot into a ballot box that was locked. Despite all of the new voting technology, there are still some small towns across the country that rely on the paper ballot system.

It's especially helpful for people who either won't be in their town or city on election day or aren't physically able to travel to a precinct. They fill out a paper ballot a number of

Ballot box used to count paper ballots in New Bedford, MA, c. 1920.

days before the election, mail it in or bring it to a town or city hall. It's called an "absentee ballot."

Mechanical Lever Machines:

Not too long after the paper ballots were introduced, mechanical lever machines started to gain popularity all over the country, and were almost the voting standard by 1960. This clever machine had various levers on the front with a different candidate's name assigned to each lever. All of the levers were in a horizontal row and when the voter made his or her selection, the lever was pulled down to vote. There was another, much larger lever on the machine that, when pulled, would close a curtain for privacy. When the voter would be ready to leave, he or she would operate the larger lever again, the curtain would open, and all of the voting levers would automatically return to their original positions.

Punch Cards:

In 1964, punch cards were first debuted in a primary in Georgia. On the punch card, next to the candidate's name, is a tiny rectangle to punch out with a pin device. After the voter makes his or her choice, the card is then either put into a box or fed into a computer. The little piece of paper that the pin pushes through is called a "chad." When a chad isn't cleanly eliminated from the punch cards, many varying terms describe the unclear result. Hanging, pregnant, swinging, and dimpled chads became infamous in the 2000 Presidential race between Vice President Al Gore and Texas Governor George Bush. A historically unusual recount was done in the state of Florida, because some chads revealed incompletely or partially punched holes, which were not counted by the tabulating machines.

My friend, Senator Rodrigues, had an experience with hanging chads on his first, close election. He explained that his first election was during the days of punch card voting, before electronic voting. He had hanging chads on some punch cards, so they all had to be counted by hand to see if there was a legitimate attempt to vote for someone. As he explained, "So if you wanted to vote for me and you pushed the pin in and it didn't completely remove the chad, that still counted as a vote, because it was clear intent on behalf of the voter to vote for that person, but the machine didn't pick it up. It certainly reinforced to me how important every vote is."

Optical scanner.

The Marksense Voting System:

Introduced in the 1990s, the newest voting system is called "direct recording electronic." It is basically a high-tech version of the mechanical lever system. Instead of a lever being assigned to each candidate, the choices are on the front of the machine. Voters make their selection by touching a screen, a push-button, or a similar device. The votes are recorded digitally and stored in the machine via a cartridge or smartcard.[4]

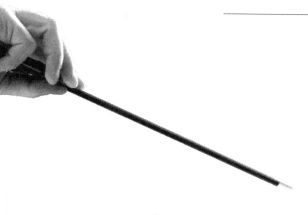

CHAPTER 19

COUNTDOWN

If American women would increase their voting turnout by ten percent, I think we would see an end to all of the budget cuts in programs benefiting women and children.
Coretta Scott King

Sixteen days before the illusion premiere, the structural truss arrived. The production team, under the direction of my longtime assistant and lighting designer, Marc Leblanc, consisted of about 10 people. Erecting the structural truss was like putting together a giant tinker toy contraption. The assembling process took about eight hours. It was exciting and nerve-wracking at the same time, seeing the physical illusion represent my dream in front of my eyes.

Next, into the late hours of the evening, and the next night as well, the lighting had to be hung on the truss. Steve Zakszewski, my technical director, was trying desperately

Illusion being erected.

to figure out the dimmers for the lighting. Steve had taken special lessons to operate a state-of-the-art lighting board that could control conventional theatrical lighting as well as all the LED and computerized robotic lights. Things weren't going well in his lighting world. He discovered a damaged dimmer and trouble with the huge generator the city had brought in. The next day, the dimmer and generator were replaced. It wasn't an easy task to replace the generator because the city only had a few of them and they were being used in other locations. But fortunately, with some creative shuffling from a sympathetic city official, we ended up with a replacement in time for the first evening rehearsal.

Meanwhile, my good friend Bill and his work crew came and lined the entire fenced-in area of about six hundred feet with black industrial fabric, to block the public's view of the rehearsals. Thank goodness for great friends. His mechanical expertise came in so handy for this massive project. He was always there, night after night, just to make sure there were no glitches. He also made sure the generator was running well and had enough gasoline to get us through the evening.

Every morning the animal keepers would bring Abner and Emily to the illusion site to familiarize them with the contraption. It was like a huge Jungle Gym to them. Emily loved to investigate it with her trunk. Bales of hay were placed around the illusion area for the animals, to create an inviting experience for them. They associated eating and playing with their hay as being a fun activity when they were around the illusion area for the animals.

Steve Zakszewski, Lyn's technical director, absorbed with the lighting equipment.

Abner scoping out the illusion site

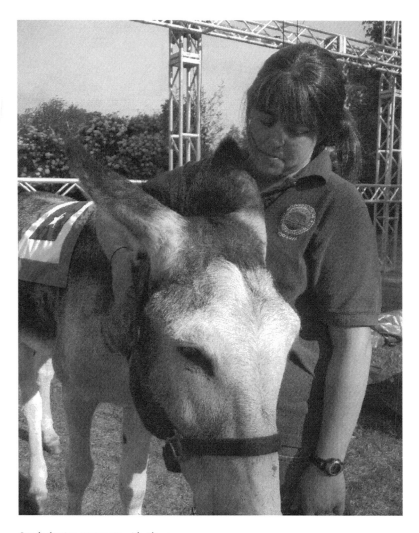

Sarah sharing a moment with Abner.

CHAPTER 20

OUR VERY FIRST REHEARSAL

Those who stay away from the election think that one vote will do no good: 'Tis but one step more to think one vote will do no harm.

Ralph Waldo Emerson

Well, it was the first night of the illusion rehearsal. None of us knew what to expect. We didn't use any lights for the first week and didn't use any music for a few days. We started with each animal individually, and very slowly lowered the framework without any fabric hanging. The next evening was the same. The third evening we slowly introduced Emily and Abner in the framework. It was the first time they were both produced! Although it was clumsy and as slow as a turtle, they both appeared without being too anxious! We were off to a very positive start.

We repeated the same sequence numerous times in a row. Each time it got slightly better. It was a great sign. After every time the illusion was performed, we'd take a break and let the animals unwind. My team had to roll up all of the sides of the canvas on the frame and make sure the ropes were tied in a certain way for me to release them. I had brought in my dear friend, professional magician David Oliver, to be our magic consultant and extra set of eyes for the illusion. Because my crew was so integral to the routine and I was involved in presenting the illusion, it was really helpful for David to give us his input and perspective on certain "magical" things. We were all so engrossed in it, we couldn't look at it from the audience's view. I did tape it every night with a camcorder but it still wasn't the same as seeing it live in real time. David was really invaluable and a great support.

The next evening the music was introduced on low volume. Before I knew it, we had the lights up and the speed was increasing. The next night the music was louder and everything was slowly starting to gel. We found that one of the problems with Abner was that he didn't like anything moving around him. It made it difficult to get him into the most optimum position for the production of the animals, but I knew I had to compromise. Knowing my time constraint, I had to settle for the placement of the animals in a way that they could get used to on a consistent basis. But, no matter what their configuration was, it was still mind-blowing!

Lo and behold, on one of our more challenging rehearsal nights I spotted a praying mantis making circles around Abner! It landed on the illusion frame. This was completely unexpected and, I thought, especially strange for a praying mantis to come out at night. Its arrival instantly reminded me of a time when my father was really ill, a few months before he passed away, and I saw a praying mantis perched on the hood of my car. That day I drove to visit a friend 10 miles away. I came home to pick up my mom to take her on errands. That same afternoon, driving down the highway, I couldn't help but notice that the praying mantis was now on the windshield! It had somehow clung to my car all of those hours. Its little antennas would whoosh in the wind as I made a turn. I tried so hard not to drive too fast for fear it would be harmed. It was pretty incredible. I kept wondering what was really going on with my special new "friend." Just as mysteriously as it appeared, it disappeared later that afternoon.

I want to share a very personal note. I had asked my father to send me a sign after he passed away to let me know he was okay. The morning after he died, my mother and I were about to drive to the funeral home. As I was backing out of our garage, I looked at a pick-up truck that was parked in my neighbor's driveway, and on the hood of the truck was a metal replica of a praying mantis.

And now, fast-forward over the years, a praying mantis appears on the rigging of my most ambitious illusion ever.

One morning after a rehearsal, I learned from my assistant Marc that he and Steve had been locked out of the zoo the evening before. The night security guard didn't realize they were still working on the illusion in the dark, and so he locked all of the gates. The team had to find a way to scale a 10-foot fence. Thank goodness they were okay and didn't have to spend the night in the zoo. What a story that would be!

There weren't enough hours in the day the last week leading up to the premiere—and not enough Lyns to go around, it seemed. But somehow things were getting done and shaping up. We had planned on filming the illusion the night before the event. We wanted to have back-up footage just in case there was a glitch when it was done live. Because of the complex nature of the illusion, it would have been impossible for a live do-over.

That evening, Hurricane Gustav was making a final pass of the Southcoast. There were substantial wind gusts and it rained hard all evening long without letting up. As much as we hated to, we not only had to cancel the filming, but the rehearsal as well. It was highly disappointing, but fortunately, on the previous evening, the animals, the trainers, my crew. and my assistants nailed it every time. And, of course, to add to the anxiety and drama of the storm, our immediate concern was to be able to check for any wind or rain damage to the illusion, lighting and sound equipment.

YOUR VOTE IS MAGIC!

CHAPTER 21

THIS IS REALLY IT

Our Presidential race is beginning to sound more and more like Harry Potter's duel with the Ministry of Magic.
Dave Beard, 2008 during the Obama/McCain Race

September 13: It came as no surprise to have the familiar feeling of butterflies in my stomach when I woke up that morning. It happens when I have a really important show that day or evening. (Between us, I always feel that way right before I'm introduced for the performance too.) I knew it was going to be a "doozey" of a day and that I had to be ready for anything. As much as I wanted everything to be absolutely perfect, and had worked toward that goal, I knew that with all of the variables involved, it was unrealistic to expect perfection. I didn't want to be a disillusioned illusionist! My grandfather gave me wonderful advice when he taught me how to play the violin. His advice really applies to any performer. He said, "Never be too confident and never take anything for granted." And I never have.

We found out that there was no major damage from the storm! However, the threat of rain was looming for most of the day. There was a constant mist in the air. You could wring out the air like a sponge. It was on our minds every second, because if it rained we wouldn't be able to do the illusion. I couldn't even think about that possibility. We were constantly checking the weather on cell phones, and the staff was on the internet throughout the day. Every minute was taken up with lots of details involving placement of staging and exhibitor tables, decorating, setting up one thousand chairs, handling politicians' campaign managers calling about lo-

Lyn's assistant Marc Leblanc, readjusts lighting instruments on the Your Vote Is Magic! canvas.

gistics, food vendors showing up, etc. It was a "zoo" within a Zoo!

We breathed a collective, big sigh of relief when it started to dry out by late afternoon. The weather forecasts weren't 100% confident that it wouldn't sprinkle a little, but we knew we could deal with a few sprinkles if need be.

One of the co-hosts, Ellen Ratner arrived in the afternoon for a private tour of the Zoo. It was such a thrill to meet her. Immediately she asked if I knew of anyone who could style her hair before the rally began. We had all of ninety minutes to work with. I called my hair stylist, Linda, and she was able to fit Ellen in at the end of her work day. This was truly a small miracle, and yet it was another reminder of some of the special people in my life. Great! That was done. But then Ellen actually got lost driving back to the Zoo! Was anything going to be easy?

The day was going by at lightning speed. It felt like time was just evaporating into a black hole. Every element of the event started to converge in the late afternoon. The press, the politicians, all the radio personalities, the brass bands, the veterans, the scouts, the volunteers—everyone—started to arrive. There was such excitement and energy in the air! The film crew arrived as well. We needed to wait until it was almost dark to do some more lighting adjustments and a few more run-throughs. I couldn't believe this was really The

Girl Scout Troup #2268. Members held up signs at the traffic intersection to promote the event and gave out Your Vote Is Magic! buttons to attendees.

Night! after the past year of planning.

Mayor Lang welcomed the audience and kicked off the town hall meeting that was part of the rally. My co-hosts, Ellen Ratner, and Ken Pittman, accompanied by Phil Paleologos, also a talk radio host of WBSM - AM 1420 took over. They did a great job of leading the audience in a question-and-answer session about voting issues. Then some of the politicians, who were incumbents or running for office, spoke to the crowd about the importance of voting. Of course, the most effective speech was given by then-Representative Michael Rodrigues. He spoke from his heart and from first-hand experience, colorfully describing his first election and

Senator Michael Rodrigues speaking to the rally crowd about his first election experience.

Ken Pittman, Ellen Ratner and Phil Palealagos conduct a town hall meeting about voting.

how close the vote was.

I'm not a fan of last minute tweaking, but because of the weather setbacks, we had no choice. We tweaked until the very last minute we could. I then had to make a difficult decision. Do we rehearse with the animals one more time?

The "worry side" of me kicked in because we weren't able to rehearse the night before. Continuity is critical with an illusion like this. Some members of my team thought we should. Some didn't. After heavy thought, I opted not to, because I didn't want Emily and Abner to be confused. They would have had to come out from their barns and then be

Some of Lyn's volunteers carefully rolling the canvas on the metal frame for the big illusion night.

brought back and come out again. It would have been different from all of the other nights. I didn't want to stray from their routine. So we did a run-through without the animals, and I just had to have faith that it would go as brilliantly as it had two nights before. I knew the animals might be more anxious because they could probably feel the energy in the air and the nervousness of the trainers. Both species are very sensitive animals.

I had one of the maintenance men from the Zoo take me to the building where I was to get ready. Because of so many unexpected last minute details, I only had about fifteen minutes to make myself look presentable, which is less than half the time I normally allow to get in "show mode." It certainly wasn't the way I wanted this to go. I wanted at least thirty minutes so I could be in "the zone" and have a few minutes to mentally run through everything. My plan was to be completely ready by the time we let the crowd into the area. But as I was taken to the building, I could hear the crowd making their way to the site. Almost one thousand people were corralled into a holding area and then they were escorted to the illusion site. I had a walkie-talkie with me to keep in touch. The timing for the next fifteen minutes was critical. And, of course, the majority of the crowd had no idea what they were about to witness. They thought this was just another part of the Your Vote Is Magic! rally. It was a stressful time for my volunteers, as they had to hurry the crowd members along in an orderly manner to the illusion site. Everyone worked in unison, including the animals. If the process took any longer than fifteen minutes, Emily and Abner could have become vocal. Trumpeting and braying noises would certainly lessen the impact! Again, the element of surprise is key to the success of any illusion.

I went to the building where the restrooms were located, and was taken aback to see about ten people in there milling around. It was supposed to be completely empty so I'd have privacy, and not have to worry about anyone barging into the ladies room as I was getting ready. Of all the silly things to fall through the cracks! I didn't have a minute to spare to call Security, so I dashed into the ladies room to get "magical," and hoped for the best as I fixed my hair, touched up my make-up, and quickly changed into costume. As an extra precaution, I threw all of my bags on the floor close to the door, to hopefully block someone from coming in. I felt like a crazy person in there, throwing clothes around, tossing make-up on the counter. It was like an "I Love Lucy" skit. And it was so humid out, it definitely wasn't a good hair night! (At that moment I could have used my "Saw The Lady In Half" Illusion on myself so I could be in two places at once.)

Everything outside of the building was organized chaos. I could hear every cue and countdown on my walkie-talkie.

Every element seemed to be going well— except for the illusionist in a complete tizzy in the ladies room! As I was applying the finishing touches, I did a mental run-through of the illusion. I took a deep breath and tried to remain calm and focused. A year of planning would be over in about two minutes! Five minutes to go. . . ."Lyn, are you ready?"

CHAPTER 22

THE ILLUSION IS REALITY

The future of this republic is in the hands of the American voter.

Dwight D. Eisenhower

Meanwhile, Emily was very excited that this was the big night. It was obvious she sensed the presence of the crowd and the electricity in the air. Plus the lighting was a little different and the music seemed a little louder. She knew the routine because we had practiced it so many times and she was anxious to go. She just wanted to hurry up and do it.

Very calmly, Emily's trainer, Jenny, kept repeating, "Emily, you've got to wait here, you have to stay here. You have to stay right here." When she was in her "magical" place before the program began, Emily could definitely hear all the activity going on. Jenny became a little bit nervous about that because it was becoming hard to get Emily not to touch things with her trunk and just be still. To keep the interaction positive for Emily, instead of putting her favorite treat, grapes, in her mouth—which allowed her trunk to wander—Jenny put the grapes in her trunk, so she'd have to put her trunk in her mouth. This kept her happily occupied. Emily instinctively knew that the crowd was going to adore her so she was probably thinking, "Come on, I want my applause and more grapes!"

I heard my assistant Marc radio, "We're ready, we've got to go." I replied, "I'm on my way!" One of the zoo's maintenance men gave me a ride on a motorized cart and I arrived alongside the crowd. I radioed that I was there so Marc could give Phil Paleologos, from WBSM radio, the cue for my introduction. In his wonderful, commanding voice, he introduced me.

It was such a great feeling to hear the powerful fanfare music. The crowd was screaming as I walked over to the illusion. A member of the crew handed me the microphone and I welcomed the crowd. I was hoping my microphone wouldn't pick up the sound of my heart beating so loudly! After I thanked everyone for coming, I said, "To celebrate our freedom to vote, I've created something a little special to show that we all have the power to make a difference!" The audience saw the illuminated structure impeccably decorated with gorgeous lighting and patriotic three-dimensional stars. The audience could see through it on all four sides. It

After Lyn's introduction, she welcomes the crowd and introduces the illusion.

really looked like a first-class Vegas production.

My crew was lined up on the inside of the structure standing ready for their cues. Suspended sixteen feet in the air was a four-sided metal frame. On each side of the frame was a piece of canvas fabric tightly rolled up. There were ropes attached to each canvas. On the precise hit in the music I proceeded with my choreography. At that point, I was thinking to myself, *This is really it Lyn. There's no turning back now! Just stay calm and believe in yourself, the animals and your team.*

I grabbed the ropes for the first piece of canvas, pulled and the curtain came down without a hitch. *Whew, one down, three to go!* Every second of the presentation felt like a minute in the sense that, at any time, ANYTHING could have gone wrong. Then I walked over to the next set of ropes, pulled, and V*OILA!* the next curtain unrolled. *Half way there* . . . walked over to the other side, pulled the next set, and BAM, the next side of canvas unfurled. Now for the front canvas... the most critical one. I walked over to the two front ropes, pulled, it released and fell perfectly. Hand-painted on the front canvas in large letters were the words Your Vote Is Magic!

Each member of my crew then rushed to each side of the canvas and tied the sides together to create an enclosed rectangular canvas box. Now, for the biggest moment we were all holding our breath over. I delivered my message: "You don't have to be a magician to create change. No matter who you choose, your vote is *MAGIC*!" and simultaneously the entire canvas box lowered to the ground, revealing Emily and Abner! The crowd stood up and cheered as the animals were produced! There they were, happy as could be, like it was just a walk in the park. It was such a celebratory moment for everyone! Everything went flawlessly. Sarah, and Jenny were beaming! Even Emily and Abner seemed overjoyed. As I petted Emily, she handed me the American flag she was holding in her trunk! It was priceless! That was something we hadn't even rehearsed!

When we finished, I walked over to my mother and gave her a big hug. We both cried and she said, "Daddy would be so proud." In my heart I felt that he was with us and that every single moment of my journey was worthwhile. The funny thing was, Emily and Abner actually didn't mind being within a foot of one other! The symbolism was clear. They proved that a Democrat and Republican can get along in a confined space, put aside their differences AND work together.

After the illusion was completed, when I asked Sarah, Kay and Jenny how they felt during the illusion, Sarah replied, "Jenny and I were both a little nervous. We knew that as much as we went over it, we're still working with animals and even though they were trained, they could be unpredict-

Lyn pulls a set of ropes, releasing first curtain.

Lyn releases second curtain.

Lyn releases third curtain.

After Lyn releases the front curtain, she announces, "You don't have to be a magician to create change, no matter who you choose, your vote is Magic!"

able. If Emily decided she wasn't going to do it, she wasn't going to do it."

Kay felt, "I thought it was wonderful, it was exciting. It was a really neat and unique opportunity for me. I wasn't too nervous because I thought we practiced enough that all would go well." Jenny said, "As far as the animal behavior went, everything was perfect. We just didn't want to mess it up. We wanted to make sure it went as perfectly as it had gone in practice. We just wanted to hit it because there was no do-over." Well, they hit it alright. It was a historic moment in magic that we will never forget.

I was so incredibly proud of Emily and Abner, the trainers, my assistant Marc, my technical director Steve, and my

A miracle has happened!

wonderful crew. Also enormous thanks to Judy, David Oliver, Bill Webster, Dave Lebeau and all of the volunteers. It was an extraordinary experience and a privilege to work with such committed, devoted people coming together for such an important message. Of course, I owe a huge debt of gratitude to my family and friends for all of their love, support, and continued belief in me. It would not have happened without them and certainly not without my father's inspiration!

Later that fall, I was honored to receive a citation from the City of New Bedford for increasing voter registrations. There were 80 new registrations a day. Mayor Lang called it a phenomenon.

Oh, by the way, on November 5, Fernando Garcia deactivated the Ford Mustang's alarm, took out the box and handed it to WBSM talk show personality Evan Rousseau. The box was unlocked and my prediction was taken out of the clear tube and read by Evan. In my handwriting it stated that Senator Barack Obama will win the election by seven million votes and 350 electoral votes. That's magic, folks!

My work is far from over. My profound hope is to continue to spread the message about the importance of voting, particularly to students and first-time voters. I hope, in my way, to inspire a lifelong appreciation of the privilege and precious right we Americans are lucky enough to enjoy.

As I'm wrapping up the writing of this book, I'm so

pleased to report that both "mascots" are doing well. Abner still lives in Dover, MA, with his owner, Judy, and is thoroughly enjoying life. Emily is in great health and loves hanging out with her gal pal Ruth every day. She receives lots of attention and love from her adoring, dedicated keepers.

Abner and Emily's brief but memorable career in show business is forever celebrated in the video that can be seen online at www.yourvoteismagic.com.

Until we see each other again (and you never know where I'll appear!), don't forget . . . your vote is . . . MAGIC!

Lyn's illusion is reality!

Endnotes

1. Abramson, Sam. "Why are a donkey and an elephant the symbols of the Democratic and Republican Parties?" 07 April 2008. HowStuffWorks.com. <http://www.history.howstuffworks.com/american-civil-war/donkey-elephant.htm> 12 January 2012

Decision America: 2010 Elections Last Updated: Mar 15, 2011 <http://libguides.fau.edu/content.php?pid=114550&sid=1322261> 16 December 2011

Running for Office: Candidates, Campaigns, and the Cartoons of Clifford Berryman, <http://www.archives.gov/press/press-kits/berryman-cartoons/berryman-bio.html>24 February 2012

2. Blake, Aaron. "The 2012 Iowa caucuses and the 10 closest races in history" January 4, 2012 < http://www.washingtonpost.com/blogs/the-fix/post/the-2012-iowa-caucuses-and-the-10-closest-races-in-history/2012/01/04/gIQAloL4aP_blog.html>. 12 February 2012

<http://www.digitalhistory.uh.edu/database/article_display.cfm?HHID=649> 15 February 2012

Forer, Ben Small Margins - A Look Back At The Closest Votes January 4, 2012 http://abcnews.go.com/blogs/politics/2012/01/small-margins-a-look-back-at-the-closest-votes/ 10 February 2012

Florida's Elections Division: Every Vote Counts <http://abcnews.go.com/Politics/story?id=121726&page=2#.T99JNZHAETA> 20 January 2012

Mitt Romney Wins Iowa Caucus Results 2012, 14 January 2012

<http://www.huffingtonpost.com/2012/01/04/mitt-romney-iowa-caucus-results-2012_n_1181822.html> 18 January 2012

Reagle, Chris. Wicked Local Rochester, Lackluster election produces some excitement with narrow one vote victory 12 April 2012 <http://www.wickedlocal.com/rochester/news/x1830129975/Lackluster-election-produces-some-excitement-with-narrow-one-vote-victory#axzz1y9mGtu2P>14 April 2012

TakeBackTheHouse <https://secure.actblue.com/list/Colorado7th> 11 February 2012

Elections Commission, City of New Bedford, Massachusetts

3. <http://www.history.com/topics/voting-rights-act> 14 February 2012

<http://www.iwantmyvote.com/recount/history/> Cobb-LaMarche 2004 Vote Recount 14 November 2011

Doris Stevens, Jailed for Freedom (New York: Boni and Liveright, 1920), 369.

Schultz, Connie. A Short History Lesson on the Privilege of Voting And You Think it's a Pain to Vote, The Plain Dealer, February 19, 2004

<http://www.suffragistmemorial.org/History.html> 18 November 2011

4. <http://www./americanhistory.si.edu/vote/votingmachine.html> 14 February 2012

"ballot." The Columbia Encyclopedia, 6th ed.. 2011. Encyclopedia.com. 15 January 2012

Bellis, Mary. "The History of Voting Machines." <http://inventors.

about.com/library/weekly/aa111300b.htmttp> 12 January 2012

Cherokee Clans, <http://www.search.com/reference/Clans> February 10, 2012

Elections Commission, City of New Bedford, Massachusetts

Jones, Douglas. "Vote: The Machinery of Democracry". THE UNIVERSITY OF IOWA Department of Computer Science

<http://www.divms.uiowa.edu/~jones/voting/index.html> 14 January 2012

Research Sources

The following are the sources of the photos and illustrations in this book. All have been used with permission of the copyright holder or are in the public domain.

Clifford Berryman
Collection of The United States Senate, Center for Legislative Archives

Lyn Dillies Photo Collection

Still photos of the event and illusion: John Robson Photographs

The New York Times Photo Archives

Thomas Nast Illustrations
Library of Congress, Print and Photograph Collection

Women of Protest: Photographs from the Records of the National Women's Party. Manuscript Division, Library of Congress, Washington, D.C.

Woman's Suffrage Photographs: National Archives; Library

Suggested Reading

Alice Paul Institute
www.alicepaul.org

Buttonwood Park Zoo
www.bpzoo.org

Democratic Party Website
www.democrats.org

League of Women Voters
www.lwv.org

League of Women Voters Education Fund
www.vote411.org

Project Vote Smart
www.votesmart.org

Republican Party Website
www.gop.com

Rock The Vote
www.rockthevote.com

Save Your Ass Long Ear Rescue
www.saveyourassrescue.org

Turning Point Suffragist Memorial
www.suffragistmemorial.org

About the Author

Lyn Dillies is one of a handful of female illusionists in the world. She has received several awards, including the International Magicians Society's Merlin Award, the Parent's Choice Award, and the Dove Foundation Award, for her high standards in family entertainment. A pioneer in her field, Lyn has made magic history with her impressive work with elephants. She created "Magic At The Symphony," a unique program that combined her illusions with classical music played by a full symphony orchestra. Lyn also produced "Learn Magic With Lyn," a nationally acclaimed DVD that teaches children magic. Known for her magic with a message, Lyn loves to transcend her magic beyond the stage to enlighten and enrich people's lives. She hopes to accomplish this with her latest achievement, *Your Vote Is Magic!*

To learn more about Lyn, visit her websites:

www.magicoflyn.com

www.magicatthesymphony.org

www.yourvoteismagic.com

*Lyn, sharing a triumphant moment with her elephant friends, Emily and Ruth.
photo credit: Robert E. Klein*

YOUR VOTE IS MAGIC!